Well, I'll be Deemed!

Well, I'll be Deemed!

PETER DOBEREINER

Illustrated by

IONICUS

AURUM PRESS

For Zoe

First published in Great Britain 1996
by Aurum Press Ltd, 25 Bedford Avenue,
London WC1B 3AT

A catalogue record for this book is available
from the British Library

ISBN 185410 439 X

2 4 6 8 10 9 7 5 3 1
1997 1999 2000 1998 1996

Printed in Great Britain by
Hartnolls Ltd, Bodmin

CONTENTS

1. A Fine Mess They've Got Us Into   1

2. Hoist with His Own Massey Ferguson   7

3. The Case for Carrying an Abacus   12

4. When we say, 'Bitten by the Golf Bug ...'   17

5. Immovable Mobility or Mobile Immovability   23

6. Golf Sometimes Needs a Little Light Relief   28

7. An Ill Outside Agency Blows No One
   Any Good   33

8. I Remember the Face but I Don't Recall
   the Ball   38

9. We Ourselves are the Little Things Sent
   to Try Us   44

10. Nearest to the Flag but Farthest from
    the Hole   49

11. Absolutely Guaranteed: An Extra 11.3 Yards   54

12. Don't Bend or Break Me; I'm Fixed and
    Growing   59

13. Does my Bonny Lie Over the Lateral
    Water Hazard?   65

14. A Rare Case of the Fan Hitting the What?   70

15. Man the Golfer, or Man the Open-Cast Miner?   75

16. The Best Drops in Life are Free   81

17. What Do You Think You are Playing at?   86

18. For those in Peril on the Water Hazard   92

19. Idle Dalliance with Unplayable Rule Book   98

20. A Rare Bit of How's-yer-Father Interruptus   105

21. The Slippery Slope to Perdition   111

22. The Turning of the Worm   116

A FINE MESS THEY'VE GOT US INTO

Dear Chairman,

I regret that I cannot advise you of the result of my fourth-round match with Mr Culpeper as we have been unable to agree on the outcome.

In order to make caddying an economic proposition the club has decreed, as you know, of course, that each caddie shall carry two bags and receive two fees. The result of this innovation has been that caddying has again become a worthwhile occupation and caddies are freely available at the club, except for the period of their weekly migration down to the Department of Health and Social Services to collect their unemployment benefit cheques.

In a spirit of cooperation with this arrangement – carrying double, I mean, not the dole fiddle – we engaged a single caddie, 'Cougher' Hawkins, to carry both our bags. We mutually agreed that for legal purposes Hawkins should be deemed to be 'opponent's caddie' so far as I was concerned when he was expressly attending to duties for Culpeper, and vice versa.

Having given us our selected clubs, Hawkins went ahead and stood by the first green. Unfortunately my left foot slipped just as I was starting my downswing and, to the astonishment of both of us, I hit an absolute purler. The ball, descending from a great height, landed on Hawkins' head and was deflected out of bounds.

Culpeper claimed the hole on the grounds that

the ball had been deflected by my caddie. Since Hawkins at the time had been leaning against the fence smoking a cigarette, I insisted that his status at the moment of impact must have been either 'opponent's caddie' or possibly, stretching a point, an outside agency.

Culpeper dismissed my suggestion of an outside agency since the terms of our agreement specified that Hawkins should be either 'player's caddie' or 'opponent's caddie' according to the circumstances prevailing at any given time. Culpeper further argued that he couldn't conceivably be 'opponent's caddie' since I was in play at that moment while he, Culpeper, was standing idly alongside the tee offering up prayers that my ball might be blown away into the next county.

In that case, I reminded Culpeper, he was deliberately attempting to influence the movement of his opponent's ball and was liable to instant disqualification under Rule 1-2. A compromise was required. I concurred with Culpeper's *caveat* that the issue be put to the Committee at the earliest possible moment for arbitration. He hit a poor tee shot, short of the green.

As we walked forward we saw Colonel Fitzroy's spaniel pick up my ball, jump over the fence and drop the ball beside Hawkins, who had gone down like a sack of potatoes and was now spreadeagled in the bunker.

Culpeper remarked that it was important to establish, first of all, whether Hawkins was alive. If he were not fixed or growing, i.e. dead, he would be a loose impediment and I could not move him. On the other hand, if he were still breathing he would be a caddie, immaterial whether mine or his, and presumably could be lifted out of the hazard without penalty. I could see through Culpeper's little game. He wanted to go trampling in the bunker, making my lie impossible with his footprints, while ostensibly giving mouth-to-mouth resuscitation. I expressly forbade him to set foot in the sand.

On arrival at the scene we observed that the ball

had lodged against Hawkins' right shin, just at the point where his artificial leg was attached to his stump. Obviously the prosthesis was a man-made object, and therefore I could remove it as a movable obstruction. Culpeper agreed, provided I could remove it without touching any part of the loose impediment which was Hawkins.

My philosophy in tricky golfing situations has always been: when in doubt, play it as it lies. I felt a certain diffidence in selecting my sand-wedge and shuffling my feet into the sand to create a secure footing because I feared Hawkins might have expired and I had no stomach for mutilating a corpse. That would be most disrespectful. You can imagine the relief and deep satisfaction I felt when Hawkins emitted a shriek of agony as my club-head caught him a solid crack on the knee on my follow-through.

Meanwhile Culpeper was having problems of his own. After hacking his way all over the place he pitched into a puddle on the green and the nearest point of relief, as we both agreed, was on the temporary tee of the second hole. He picked up his ball and then, in defiance or ignorance of the provisions of Rule 25, he *dropped* it on the tee. I blame myself, Mr Chairman, for not informing him that in taking relief from abnormal ground conditions on the green the ball must be lifted and *placed*, but I was distracted by the dreadful groans coming from the bunker. Worse followed. He put his ball on a tee peg and putted it with a lofted stroke clear over the sheet of casual water and into the hole for a seven.

According to my reckoning I also scored seven. My sporting instincts forbade me from raising the matter of Rule 25 in detail and thereby possibly putting him off his tee shot on the second. I simply remarked casually 'My hole' and then, in due season as we were walking up the next fairway, explained my reasons for claiming the hole, namely that he had failed to rectify his wrong procedure under Rule 25 before driving off on the next hole. He replied that no claim could be entertained after we had left the green. I responded

'… when in doubt, play it as it lies.'

that the words 'My hole' constituted a claim. He reminded me that he had a prior claim to the hole. The score at this stage was therefore: either I was 1 up or 1 down, or either he or I was disqualified, or we were all square.

While we were debating these permutations, the match behind us caught us up. The club captain was amongst those present and in a vile temper. He flatly refused to entertain our explanation that our progress had been unduly delayed by our humanitarian action in going to the Fitzroys' cottage and asking Mrs Fitzroy to phone for an ambulance to collect poor Hawkins. It was the very least we could do. It wasn't as if we had hung around waiting for the ambulance to arrive.

The captain would hear none of it. As a member of the Competitions Committee, he demanded that Culpeper and I both penalise ourselves the loss of one hole for unduly delaying play. He then insisted that we stand aside while his group took the tee and played through. As a result of this intervention, I was now either 1 down, 2 down, all square or disqualified, and so, in every respect, was Culpeper.

It is amazing how shared adversity draws people together, like the blitz during the war. Culpeper and I had been somewhat at odds with each other but now we united in a spirit of fraternal solidarity against the common foe. At every subsequent point of contention we simply recited in unison: 'Shall we call it a half?' and pressed on. On one hole there was a disparity of eight strokes between our scores, but owing to a slight *contretemps* on the green when Culpeper's hearing aid fell out of his ear and might or might not have hit his ball, we refrained from all discussion on whether this object constituted a player's equipment or an artificial aid, or whether the ball had moved position or merely oscillated, or whether that distinction only applied when addressing the ball. We called it a half and in the same manner halved all the remaining holes in a spirit of warm comradeship.

I do apologise, Mr Chairman, for the delay in presenting this submission but I picked up a stinker of a cold at Hawkins' funeral and have been laid up in bed. We hope you are able to achieve a judgment in this matter without having to refer our case to the Rules of Golf Committee. After all, they are the ones who got us into this mess in the first place.

Yours faithfully,

Jas. Pontifex

2

HOIST WITH HIS OWN MASSEY FERGUSON

Dear Chairman,

You will know all about the accident which befell the greenkeeper who was mowing the grass around our pot bunker on the first hole, which is designated by the more mealy-mouthed members as the 'Devil's Navel'. Apparently the turf around the edge of the bunker gave way under the weight of the tractor which toppled into the murky depths of that benighted bunker. We must be thankful that the driver did not sustain more serious injuries. At all events the removal of the tractor clearly posed a considerable problem and it was still there, almost filling the cavernous aperture, when we teed off for the monthly medal. As ill chance would have it, Mr Culpeper's drive was slightly pulled and his ball rolled into the bunker, coming to rest in the tread of the tractor's near-side rear tyre where it was clearly unplayable but easily accessible.

Culpeper sought my guidance as to the correct relief procedure and I answered thuswise: 'In plain language you get a free drop one club's length from the point which is not nearer the hole, avoids interference from the obstruction and is *not* in a hazard, except that the ball must be dropped *in* the bunker.'

He scratched his head, wrinkled his nose and blinked rapidly, for all the world like a man who has just seen a five-legged horse trot by and fears he has lost the ability to count up to ten.

'Run that past me again, if you would be so kind.'

I did so, this time reading the exact wording of Rule 24-2b(ii) and Rule 24-2b(i). He took the Rule Book and studied the relevant passages in a state of increasing agitation.

'I have to drop *in* the bunker, not nearer the hole. Condition (a)?'

'Yes.'

'In a place which avoids interference? Condition (b)?'

'Exactly.'

'But there is nowhere in that bunker which is free from interference from the tractor.'

'Be that as it may, you must still abide by the rules.'

'And *not* in a bunker? Condition (c)?'

'Precisely. I couldn't have put it more succinctly myself.'

'So you are telling me that I am entitled to free relief if I fulfil two impossible conditions namely dropping inside and outside the bunker simultaneously, and in a place which does not exist, i.e. free from interference by the immovable obstruction?'

'Correction,' I replied. 'I am not telling you these things. The Rules of Golf are so directing you.'

A note of agitation was creeping into his voice.

'What in the name of sweet reason *can* I do?'

I reminded him that it was always pointless to invoke the name of sweet reason when trying to follow the labyrinthine peregrinations of the legal mind. We must cut the sealed knot of 24-2b(i) and (ii) with the keen blade of commonsense. I suggested that the fact that the ball was sitting there in plain view did not disqualify it, *per se,* from the status of lost ball. Then there was the further and possibly more rational option of deeming it to be unplayable. Either way it meant going back and playing three off the tee.

Culpeper became quite heated at my attempts to help him. He accused me in the most wounding terms of trying to lumber him with a penalty stroke when he was clearly entitled to a free drop.

In self defence, I had to disclaim any responsibil-

8

ity for a Rule of Golf which is patently impossible to implement.

Culpeper then tried reasonableness. His argument ran along the following lines:

The legislators quite obviously wanted him to have free relief in this situation. In drafting a Rule requiring him to drop both inside and outside the hazard simultaneously, in a place which did not actually exist, there must have been some bureaucratic cock-up or possibly a printer's error. *Ergo*, we should proceed under the old wartime adage so frequently invoked in the armed services that regulations were for the guidance of the wise and for the blind obedience of fools. As wise and reasonable men we should use our initiative and seek a compromise in the spirit of Rule 1-4: 'If any point in dispute is not covered by the Rules, the decision shall be made in accordance with Equity.' Therefore he should be allowed to drop a ball without penalty outside the bunker.

Naturally, I could not countenance any such procedure. The point in dispute *was* covered by a Rule, albeit a lunatic and self-contradictory one, so there was no scope for invoking equity. Any hanky-panky with the Rules, even the daft ones, would render us both liable for disqualification for agreeing to exclude the operation of any Rule or to waive any penalty incurred.

By this time there was quite a pile-up of players on the tee waiting for the fairway to clear so that they could start their rounds. Catcalls and shouts of open abuse urged us to get on with it.

Culpeper had been puffing furiously at a cigarette, which by this point had burnt down almost to the cork tip. He tossed this glowing remnant behind him, straight into the bunker as it happened. You will have had a report – no pun intended – on what transpired. There was an almighty explosion and the tractor rose several feet into the air before falling back into the bunker, burning ferociously.

We were both thrown to the ground by the force of the blast and when we recovered our senses and

'There was an almighty explosion ...'

upright postures we noticed Culpeper's ball sitting pretty on the grass a foot from the rim of the bunker. In short order Culpeper whacked it with his four-wood, yelled an obscene response to those abusing him from the tee, and marched hurriedly up the fairway.

Remarkably, in the light of that traumatic experience, Culpeper played a wonderful round and I warrant the enclosed card will be good enough to claim the silverware. But I am troubled in my mind, Mr Chairman, by the cigarette. You will, of course, be familiar with Decision 13-2/12 which determines that if your ball is lying on a piece of paper and you set fire to it – the paper, not the ball – then you are deemed to have improved your lie. Is exploding a tractor on which your ball lies not essentially similar, albeit on a far more heroic scale?

If you should deem that such is indeed the case then I fear Mr Culpeper's negligence in failing to add two penalty strokes to his score for the first hole must inevitably, as surely as night follows day, result in his disqualification for signing for a score lower than actually taken.

Please be assured, Mr Chairman, that in drawing this matter to your attention I have in no way been influenced by the circumstance that I scored one stroke higher than Mr Culpeper and that his elimination from the competition must therefore elevate me from second place onto the winner's rostrum.

Yours faithfully,
Jas. Pontifex

3

THE CASE FOR CARRYING AN ABACUS

Dear Chairman,

You will notice that in submitting Mr Culpeper's monthly medal card I haved added a proviso to my signature in the space designated 'Marker', as follows: 'Score subject to ratification by the committee after consideration of the attached affidavit.'

This is the aforementioned affidavit.

My friend Culpeper and I have evolved a sporting convention for use on the blind third hole. The player with the honour drives off and then proceeds directly to the brow of the hill so as to monitor the flight and destination of his opponent's drive. Over the years we must have saved countless dozens of golf balls and endless hours of searching through the heather through exercise of this simple courtesy.

On this occasion I hit off and on reaching my point of lofty vantage I saw Culpeper take an almighty thrash at his ball. The sole plate of his driver must have just grazed the top of the ball because it toppled off its peg and rolled forward about fifteen inches. The rules of etiquette forbade me from raising my voice to counsel caution as he snatched up the ball and hurled it into the pond. Waving my arms as I ran back towards the tee failed to attract his attention and he teed up another ball and hit it. Quite well, too, considering his state of mind.

'My dear chap,' I remarked on arrival at the scene, 'what on earth do you think you are doing?'

'Quite simple,' he said in rather an aggressive

'… he snatched up the ball and hurled it into the pond.'

tone. 'I could not contemplate going on living without drowning that sniggering, supercilious swine of a golf ball. So I did. Then I reloaded and hit another.'

'Under what pretext did you put another ball into play?'

'I declared the first one lost, of course.'

'You actually made a verbal announcement to that effect?'

'Obviously there was nobody here to make a declaration to. And I am not in the habit of engaging the ball-washer in idle chit chat.'

'So how then can you claim to have made a declaration?'

'It was a mental thing.'

'But in your mind you associated the two words declare and lost?'

'Certainly. I determined to deem my ball to be lost and therefore I was perfectly at liberty to play another.'

'This is one of the instances in golf when what you say is just as important as what you do. There is a problem with your wording.'

'Oh, semantics is it? Well suppose I asserted that my ball was lost? Or averred it? Or acclaimed it? Or announced it? Since it all went on inside my mind we are concerned more with intention than we are with lexicography.'

'No, the problem is that you cannot declare your ball to be lost.'

'What?'

'It is not permitted.'

'Show me the rule where it says you can't declare your ball lost.'

'It isn't in any rule.'

'Where is it then?'

'There is a Decision which says so.'

'Is there any penalty for a breach of a Decision?'

'Not as such, no. Decisions are the case law of golf. They provide valuable explanations and interpretations of the rules. Only a breach of a rule involves a penalty.'

'So you are saying I must be penalised because of an interpretation of something that is not in any rule?'

'That's about the size of it.'

'All because of a form of words. What should I have said?'

' "I deem that ball unplayable," would have done the trick. That would have taken the ball out of play and you would have been at liberty to put another ball into play.'

'So what is the situation now?'

'Well, the ball in play is now at the bottom of the pond. So you must penalise yourself for picking up a ball in play, for starters. Now the ball you hit with your second stroke was a wrong ball. Another penalty. And then there is the little matter of putting it on a tee peg. That constitutes improving your lie. Another penalty.'

'Hold on. The ball was on the tee and there is most definitely a rule which says that when you put a ball into play on the tee it may be teed.'

'A little learning is indeed a dangerous thing. The Rules of Golf do not acknowledge the existence of a tee.'

'Don't be daft. How can you possibly say that the Rules do not acknowledge tees? Dammit, there are usually four or five of them on every hole.'

'Indeed so. Nevertheless, they have no standing in the rules. Those levelled rectangles of pristine lawn which we call tees are merely "closely mown areas of through the green" so far as the Rules are concerned. Don't ask me why the Rules of Golf Committee select an adjectival clause like "through the green" to do duty as a noun but I suppose it would be too much to expect legal experts to be literate. Goodness knows, it took long enough for them to stop using the word "alternate" when they clearly meant "alternative". I digress. The point is that the rules are concerned only with the "teeing ground", a rectangle extending a club's length back from a line drawn between the markers. Your ball lay outside this "teeing ground", in a "closely mown area of through the green". So there could be no question of teeing up its replacement.

Furthermore, as I observed, you did not tee it up on that precise spot. You cast around looking for an inviting patch of turf, the way you always do on the tee, before teeing the ball.

'So, in summary, you picked up a ball in play, you wrongly declared it to be lost, you improved your lie, you played a wrong ball and you played from a wrong place. You played two strokes so I reckon justice will have been served if we walk on to that second ball and pick up play. Unless I have grossly miscalculated the tally of penalties, your next shot will be your twelfth.'

Yours faithfully,
Jas. Pontifex

4

WHEN WE SAY, 'BITTEN BY THE GOLF BUG ...'

Dear Chairman,

Now that South Africa is no longer the pariah of the international community and, under the presidency of Mr Nelson Mandela, has been restored into the family of nations as well as being welcomed by Her Majesty the Queen back into the Commonwealth, Mr Culpeper and I recently decided to enjoy a holiday in the land of the springbok. Naturally we took our sticks and had several enjoyable rounds and were delighted to observe the harmony between the races, with the white golfers and their black caddies clearly on the best of terms. But then golf has always been at the forefront of progress in matters of racial and sexual emancipation and equality. I might cite as a shining example of this enlightenment the recent decision by the Council of our own club to build a covered walkway so that our lady members shall not be incommoded in inclement weather on their way from their locker room to the toilet shed.

In enclosing our African safari cards for purposes of handicap adjustments I am obliged to draw your attention to the card from High Veld Club. As its name implies, this is an up-country club where, as we were surprised to observe, the members wear rudimentary gaiters made of lengths of car tyre. A few eyebrows were raised when Culpeper and I appeared in our tweed plus-twos, but they are a most hospitable people and they insisted on furnishing us with their regular dress of khaki shorts and those gaiters. When I voice my assumption that they were for protection against snake bites the secretary corrected me.

'No, for flora rather than fauna. They are to protect your legs against thorns and saw-grass. You have to fend off the wildlife as best you can. A good smack with your wedge will discourage most snakes and the smaller mammals.' Culpeper received this remark with a look of apprehension, but I divined that the secretary was pulling the legs he had so thoughtfully protected with radial-treaded armour.

We had black chaps to carry the bags and, apart from refusing to search for balls in the rough, they were very good. I quickly cottoned on to the reason they would not venture into the high grass, and Culpeper and I decided to treat rough as lateral water hazards, dropping a ball on the fairway under penalty of one stroke and pressing on. In view of the special circumstances I am sure you will endorse this self-inflicted temporary local rule as a prudent expedient rather than an agreement to ignore a Rule of Golf.

On the seventh hole Culpeper's drive was sliced and the ball bounced just off the fairway into the tall grass among a cluster of ant hills. These are not like our domestic ant hills, which appear puny compared with the extraordinary African structures which rise as high as twenty feet, quite amazing examples of communal cooperation and innate engineering skill. Culpeper shouted across the fairway: 'Do the Rules of Golf define the ant as a burrowing animal?' My shake of the head gave him the literal answer to his query but my verbal addendum, namely that the local rules dictated that ant hills be treated the same as immovable obstructions, apparently failed to carry to him against the breeze. He took his wedge and as he set himself for a mighty crunch his caddie skipped smartly into the centre of the fairway with a wide-eyed look of internal agitation.

To conform with the customs of the country – from my hazy boyhood memories of *Jock of the Bushveld* – I had affectionately appellated our caddies 'Boy 1' and 'Boy 2'. I asked mine: 'why is Boy 2 getting his knickers in such a twist?' He replied: 'The king cobra customarily makes its nest in an ant hill in symbiotic relationship with the *Formicidae*,' adding in a tone that to my ear, untuned to local speech patter   sounded suspiciously sarcastic: 'Baas!' No wonder he was so alarmed when Culpeper dislodged a large section of ant hill in blasting his ball back onto the fairway.

As it happened, on the next hole my ball came to rest against an ant hill. Naturally I determined the nearest point which afforded complete relief from the obstruction, on the area of closely mown grass as luck would have it, and dropped my ball. Culpeper raised a frightful stink, ranting away about locker-room lawyers getting away with blue bloody murder. With my usual patience and forebearance I quietly explained that the Rules of Golf do not require a player to put himself in a position of physical danger, viz the Decision allowing a player the option, when faced with a ball adjacent to a coiled rattlesnake in a bunker, to drop another ball in another bunker affording the same lie, distance and degree of difficulty. Furthermore, I continued, I had drawn his attention to the local rules providing relief from ant hills. He yelled back: 'You specifically indicated that the ant was not designated as a burrowing animal by the Rules of Golf!' 'Nor is it so deemed,' I replied, handing him my Rule Book to verify the veracity of my response. He said he was far from satisfied and wished the matter to be raised with the committee, hence my objective recital of the events, Mr Chairman.

I was getting used to the nappy greens by the time we reached the thirteenth green, an appropriate number in view of the unlucky occurrence which was about to transpire. I was away and trying to read my putt, which looked to me as if it would break three ways and then swerve on the nap up the steepish slope to the hole. 'How do you see it?' I enquired and, getting no reply, looked around. The scene which greeted my enquiring gaze was positively alarming. The two caddies were running full pelt back up the fairway and Culpeper was leaping about as if under the influence of some powerful stimulant, which indeed he was, as it transpired in due course. He was also crimson in the face from the exertion of not disturbing my concentration and suppressing the growing compulsion to shriek in pain. Good for him. Full marks for observing the game's etiquette despite massive provocation.

Freed from such considerations, he now screamed in agony and began tearing off his clothing. All of it. He was flapping at his body with his discarded shirt and rending the air with fearsome oaths, and my initial reaction was to conclude that my old friend was having some form of seizure, which in a way he was. I then saw the source of the problem: his body was swarming with large, black ants. Apparently, as we learned later, they were called soldier ants from their habit of marching in single file, thousands of them in an immense column of short-tempered and hungry creatures armed with mandibles which can rip into human flesh as easily as a fork plunging into a pat of butter. Culpeper had inadvertently stationed himself right on top of this marching column alongside the green and the ants had promptly marched up his leg and inside his shorts. The South Africans call these creatures 'balbijters' and when I asked the reason for this soubriquet I was told that surely it was obvious. I wasn't at all sure, since the ants showed not the slightest interest in biting Culpeper's golf ball but were clearly hellbent on consuming Culpeper.

I deemed the wisest course of action to be to assist in the process of removing the ants by flapping at them with my golf towel and did so, taking care to concentrate on the upper, or more public, areas of his person. It was an exhausting task and made the more difficult by Culpeper leaping all over the place like a madman in the throes of some kind of fit, dislodging both our golf balls in the process. Salvation arrived in the form of the automatic sprinklers which came on, thanks to our caddies raising the alarm on arrival back at the clubhouse. The subsequent dousing put the ants to flight and in short order the secretary arrived on a golf cart and took Culpeper back to the clubhouse for an injection, some soothing ointment and a change of clothing.

'… *began tearing off his clothing.*'

While awaiting his return I tried to assess how many penalty strokes Culpeper had amassed during his frenzy. Naturally enough the compelling requirement to render assistance to Culpeper had distracted me in some degree from my duties to monitor play and ensure full observance of all Rules of Golf. Culpeper had not marked and lifted his ball since it was nowhere near my line of play and I am positive that he kicked it at least four times. My ball, being furthest from the hole and therefore on the periphery of the unfolding drama was moved only three times. Rule 18 is clear in stating that a stationary ball moved by an opponent or by a player must be replaced before playing another stroke. It does not state, and this is a serious omission in my view, the procedure to be adopted in replacing the ball after multiple displacements. Do you take it straight to its original location? Or do you – and this is the method I should prefer – return it from its final resting place, which we may designate Position D, to Position C, intoning the while 'That's one penalty stroke'; and then repeat the process through Positions B and A?

I was pondering this legal dilemma when Culpeper returned. He was in a bad way and looked awful, covered in lurid blotches of ointment and walking in a most stilted manner. I simply did not have the heart to mention the penalties at the time because the poor chap had suffered enough for one day, or so I deemed. His attached card therefore has not been adjusted to accommodate the due penalties and I hope, Mr Chairman, that you will find it in the goodness of your heart to limit his sanction to the bare seven penalty strokes. In the light of the agony and the trauma of that occasion it would be heaping Pelion upon Ossa to inflict him with a disqualification for arbitrarily suspending play without a reason satisfactory to the Committee.

Yours faithfully,
Jas. Pontifex

5

IMMOVABLE MOBILITY
OR
MOBILE IMMOVABILITY

Dear Chairman,

As you know the Rules of Golf Committee is far too high and mighty to entertain queries from we individual serfs, villains and lepers who mistakenly believe that we collectively represent the very backbone of the game of golf. Only golf clubs dare approach the high table of golf to make supplications to our masters, hence I have no choice but to petition your good offices once more.

Last week Culpeper and I decided to have a day's golf down on the south coast, at a club which was busily preparing to host a major professional tournament. The place was in turmoil, I can tell you, what with all the last-minute preparations of banging in tent pegs and refrigerated trucks delivering mountains of frozen ham sandwiches. No matter. We got off bright and early and on the third hole, for some unaccountable reason, I contrived to pull my drive well left. My line to the flag was blocked by the extended arm of one of those mobile crane whatsits the BBC uses to elevate cameras high into the air. I think they're called cherry-pickers. I picked up my ball, edged sideways until I had a clear view of the green, took one more enormous stride sideways, extended my arm and dropped the ball. Fortuitously, this legal manoeuvre took me clear of the waist-high rough and I now had a perfect lie on the fairway. But then, as you know, the Rules of Golf are also the golfer's Bill of Rights and if the rules give you an advantage you should take it. Right?

Culpeper got quite shirty and asked me what the hell I thought I was doing. I told him I was taking a lawful drop. He then enquired what on earth I thought that thing was that entitled me to move my ball from the rough to the fairway. I replied with all the dignity I could muster that I did not know its official name but that to a golfer it was an immovable obstruction. Culpeper then turned sarcastic, like he does. 'Immovable? Four-wheel-drive, 200-horsepower engine, man behind the wheel, key in ignition and you have the brass cheek to call it immovable. Anyway, you don't get line of sight relief from an obstruction, immovable or not.'

Well, I had to tell him. 'Things like cranes and commentary towers are covered by special tournament rules and you most certainly get line of sight relief from them.'

Admittedly we were not participating in the tournament but common sense dictated that we had to treat these tournament intrusions under tournament rules. As for whether or not this particular item was movable or immovable we had the decision from the highest possible authority, from the very mouth of the ultimate horse in the person of the Chairman of the Rules of Golf Committee, Dr Trey Holland, who had deemed in the US Open at Oakmont that such a vehicle was an immovable obstruction. Hence he ruled that Ernie Els, who had pulled his drive into the most frightful clag, not only should, but *must*, drop his ball onto the fairway.

Culpeper took all with an ill grace, but mention of the highest authority in the world shut him up. I beat him by a stroke and he insisted on my giving him a chance to get even. So we went out again. By coincidence Culpeper hooked his drive and the ball finished in the same spot, in a slightly worse lie than mine at the bottom of a bank. My scream just stopped him in time and saved him from a penalty for picking up the ball. 'You don't get a drop from a movable obstruction,' I said.

'But you said it was an immovable obstruction,' he yelled. 'You got a free drop.'

'Yes, yes,' I explained, 'but that was the first occasion. If you remember from the television of the US Open play-off, Ernie Els drove into that same place again and this time the highest authority in the world, namely the Chairman of the Rules of Golf Committee, Dr Trey Holland, took due note of your objections about four-wheel-drive, 200-horsepower engine, driver ready and waiting to shift the blasted machine, and he re-deemed the contraption to be a movable obstruction. So go ahead and ask the drive to kindly move it out of your line of sight.'

He returned in short order, crimson with embarrassment and muttering something about the BBC being banned from the air if that sort of language ever got broadcast. He appealed to my better nature and suggested that since the driver refused to move his vehicle we should treat it as an immovable obstruction. With the best will in the world, Mr Chairman, I could not reverse the decision of the world's highest authority, could I? I was reluctantly obliged to tell Culpeper that he must play the ball as it lay.

He took an almighty thrash with his wedge and drove the ball a good three inches into the bank. But for the fear of breaching the rules of etiquette by speaking on his backswing, I would have warned him of the possible consequence of taking another crack at the ball. Too late. That second blow embedded the ball a good seven inches into the bank, leaving it totally unplayable with anything less than a front-loader.

'I'm declaring it unplayable,' he snarled.

'I think not,' I said. 'Dropping within two club-lengths not nearer the hole puts you out of bounds. The same goes for going back as far you like, keeping this spot between you and the flagstick. That just leaves returning to the spot from which you struck the last shot and that is deep inside that bank.'

Having pondered my remarks he turned on his heel and walked off in a pretty well elevated state of dudgeon.

'He took an almighty thrash ... and drove the ball
into the bank!'

ged, Mr Chairman, if you can
powers that be whether any con-
reached on whether these mobile
e mobile immovable obstructions or
obile obstructions. The ambiguity and
y of the world's highest authority on the
olf really need to be resolved once and for

nally I must apologise for the writing on the
sed card (for handicapping purposes, please) in
space delineated for the marker's signature. I can
nderstand Culpeper's reluctance, in the circumstances, to endorse my card with his signature, but his
message is quite unforgivable. It is also physically
impossible.

Yours faithfully,
Jas. Pontifex

6

GOLF SOMETIMES NEEDS A LITTLE LIGHT RELIEF

Dear Chairman,

I am sorry to trouble you again but since we are required to submit all cards, even those from away courses, for handicapping purposes, and since the 'muni' at Sodding Chipbury does not have a competitions committee, I have no other choice but to submit my problems for your wise adjudication.

As you know, nobody in the club enjoys a jolly jape more than Mr Culpeper. This was his first visit to the course and, as you are doubtless also aware, the approach to their third green is dreadfully confusing. There is no defintiion to the hole and you are looking at a positive cluster of greens ahead. Unless you know the course you might play to any one of three targets. Purely for the sake of our mutual amusement and with no vestige of malicious or nefarious intent, I privily instructed my caddie to go forward and hold up the flagstick of the seventeenth green.

Culpeper remarked that it was gratifying to note that my caddie had the sense to hold up the flag without being asked, a remark which I deemed could be deemed to indicate his authorisation. Wouldn't you just believe it? He bit an absolute corker two feet from the hole on the seventeenth green. He feigned to be miffed when he discovered his error had cost him a seven when he had been anticipating an easy three.

We both hit decent drives just short of the

marker post at the fourth hole and as we walked up to our balls he remarked that it was a really stupid mistake on the part of my caddie to hole up the wrong flag. I had a job keeping a straight face as I told him that I was responsible for this droll ploy. I added that such a joke was only possible between two such good friends as us. We were, I presumed to deem, like those heavenly twins, Castor and wassisname.

'Pollux!' said Culpeper, turning quite red in the face. 'You mean you deliberately tricked me into playing for the wrong green?'

'All in the game, old boy,' I replied, 'Fully endorsed and authorised by The Rules of Golf Committee of the Royal and Ancient Golf Club of St Andrews.' I read him the relevant Decision: 'The player may have the flagstick held up at any time.' Clear as daylight. Any time means any time. If you can have the flagstick held up at any time then obviously you can have the seventeenth flagstick held up while you are playing the third.

At this juncture my poor friend suffered some form of seizure, his face turning bright red and his right arm thrusting out in an involuntary reflex, with the fingers tightly bunched. Fortunately I have the reflexes of a cat and ducked, so the marker post behind me took the full force of the impact, which wrenched it from its socket and caused it to fall to the ground.

Now, you must know Nosher Perkins who has a secondhand car business in some ghastly place like Catford or Streatham. As it later transpired, he had lost his ball in the woods and was returning to the tee to play another. You may be further aware that he has some trick of jamming the governor on his golf cart with a pencil so it goes like the absolute clappers.

Culpeper was making such a din, hopping around in circles with both hands jammed between his thighs and screaming blue murder, that I was unaware of the approach of Perkins until his golf cart crested the brow of the hill, doing what I deemed to be about sixty. He didn't have a chance in hell of missing the

'... The marker post took the full force.'

fallen marker post, and by wrenching the wheel hard over probably made the result worse. The offside front wheel hit the post, flipping the cart over and projecting Perkins into the air as if fired on an ejector seat.

The cart rolled over and over down the hill and Perkins landed with such force as to dislodge both his dentures, wrench his colostomy bag from its spigot and fracture his collar bone in two places. I told Perkins that the mishap was entirely his own fault but he was in no mood to listen to reason, replying with a terse rejoinder. I was surprised that a man like him had even heard of Immanuel Kant; he is the last person I would suspect of familiarity with *Metaphysische Anfangsgrunde der Naturwissenschaft.*

I deemed Perkins well able to fend for himself. Anyway, the rest of his group would surely come back to see what was wrong if his reappearance was unduly delayed. I told Culpeper we should press on. You will note, Mr Chairman, that I for one have learnt my lesson about slow play.

Culpeper was all for replacing the marker post but I warned him that I would be unable to countersign his card if he did any such thing, Rule 8-2a: 'Any mark placed during the play of a hole by the player or with his knowledge shall be removed before the stroke is played.'

At that moment a small passenger plane flew over. 'How appropriate,' I remarked, putting my arm around Culpeper's shoulders, 'a friendship. I forget who makes that particular plane.'

'Fokker!' said Culpeper in a tone which anyone who did not know him might have mistaken for irritability. He tried to play his ball, holding the club with the left hand only. I had to give him an A for Effort because he really laid into the shot, but his control left a lot to be desired. He missed the ball entirely and caught himself a fearful whack on the left toe. With that he stalked off, limping and with his right hand clasped under his left armpit.

I have deemed it necessary, Mr Chairman, to relate the above incidents at some length in order that you should be able to appreciate why the enclosed card is not endorsed by a signature in the space designated: Marker.

Perforce, I had to complete the round by myself; a pity that, because I am sure Culpeper would have enjoyed and marvelled at the golf I produced thenceforth. Nine birdies, two eagles and nothing worse than par. One dreams of such rounds and one would have wished for a reliable and objective witness when one had 'one of those days'.

I shall perfectly understand if you wish to confer with the Secretary of the Ladies' Handicapping Committee, since my previous standard of play was outside the men's handicap limit. And I realise that it may be slightly unusual to go from the Bronze Division to Category One in one quantum leap. In applying to have you validate my card for handicapping purposes I remind you that you have the power in exceptional circumstances to accept a card which has not been countersigned by the marker. You will agree, I feel sure, that the circumstances in this case were indeed somewhat exceptional.

Yours faithfully,
Jas. Pontifex

7

AN ILL OUTSIDE AGENCY BLOWS NO ONE ANY GOOD

Dear Chairman,

I write to lodge a formal appeal against the disqualification of Mr Culpeper and myself in the monthly medal, which, as I feel sure you will agree when you hear the full details, was due to a ludicrous misunderstanding and without the slightest justification in golf law.

You know our new member, Freddy Holme, who bought the cottage by the practice ground previously owned by the late and much-lamented Assistant Secretary, 'Auntie', or to give her in death the full name which we never used in her lifetime, or even knew in most cases, Miss Anthea Low.

Well, Culpeper and I had a late starting time so we decided to loosen up a bit. We therefore took ourselves off to a quiet corner by the Holme home on the range where the dear Anthea (Auntie) Low played. After a bit Freddie came out and said: 'Don't wear yourselves out, chaps, come in and have a cup of coffee.' Which we did. You are probably unaware that I first met Culpeper through our mutual interest in chamber music, both of us being devotees of the *cor anglais*. I beg you to keep the next bit to yourself because we want it to be a surprise; but, between you, me and the gatepost we have made up a trio, with Freddy on the piano, and we are working up a short recital for the club's smoker on Saturday week. It

33

occurred to us that we had time for a rehearsal and after our coffee break we had a run through of our selection. Music is like golf in that practice makes perfect.

As to the round itself, we had a couple of incidents but my comprehensive knowledge of the Rules enabled me to dispose of them without much trouble. I will run them past you in any case, just so that you can confirm my rulings.

On the tee of our monstrously long seventh I told Culpeper that the trick with the wind blowing from behind was to get the ball up and flying. Accordingly I put my ball on a high tee and, in order to eliminate any chance of topping the shot, I focused on Ben Hogan's sage advice to concentrate on knocking your tee peg out of the ground. In the event my club-head went clear under the ball, which popped almost vertically into the air, a mishap which triggered Culpeper's weakness for sarcasm: 'There she blows, right up into the jet stream!'

I had the last laugh. The ball descended gently onto a trailer load of bunker sand which the green-keeper was conveying up to the green. It was one of those occasions when a thorough knowledge of the Rules can save you a stroke or two. Grabbing my wedge, I trotted behind the trailer and I was pretty well out of puff, I can tell you, as the trailer came alongside the green. I swung my wedge and deftly, if I may be so immodest as to say so, flipped the ball from its sandy lie and, for one excruciating moment, thought it was going into the hole. It stopped on the lip for the first albatross of my golfing career.

Culpeper raised an objection, namely that I should have dropped the ball as near as possible on the spot where the ball came to rest on the moving, inanimate, outside agency. Perforce I had to point out the facile, nay simplistic, error of his suggestion, adding that a little learning, in my humble opinion, was a dangerous thing. Had he but drunk more deeply at the well of knowledge he would have recognised that this situation was akin to a ball lodging in the branch of

'I ... flipped my ball from its sandy lie.'

tree waving in the wind or, to take on an even closer parallel, to a ball being borne along at fifty miles an hour in the rushing torrent of a mountain stream. In both instances, as fully documented in the book of Decisions, the ball was legally deemed to be stationary because it was not moving in relation to the branches or water which held it in thrall. In both cases the player is at liberty to play a lawful stroke at the ball without penalty. Culpeper was far from convinced by my dissertation and judgment, but by now he knows better than to argue with a recognised authority on golf law.

He cheered up when I was able to apply my legal scholarship in his favour at the short tenth. He hit a good tee shot about six feet from the flagstock and marked his ball while I did my usual Whirling Dervish act in that confounded pot bunker. Eventually Culpeper had his chance to resume play and he replaced his ball. He had retrieved his marker and was surveying the line of his putt when a particularly strong gust of wind set his ball into motion. It trickled and trickled and trickled and toppled into the hole.

'Stationary ball moved by outside agency. I replace it, right?'

'No, my dear old booby,' I replied. 'This is your birthday. Wind is not an outside agency. It has no standing in the Rules of Golf. So your ball, which you have been holding betwixt finger and thumb for ten minutes while I played out of that idiotic trap, is deemed in golf law never to have stopped moving and, as it were, to have continued its inexorable progress into the hole under the impetus of your stroke from the teeing ground.'

'Meaning?'

'Meaning drinks all round when we get in because you have just made a copper-bottomed, hallmarked on every link, guaranteed for life, as kosher as they come, genuine, perfectly legal hole-in-one.'

As you can imagine we were in chipper mood when we made it back to the clubhouse and all the more heavily gobsmacked when we handed in our cards to see the dreaded designation 'DQ' against both our names. I confronted the Secretary and demanded an explanation for this outrage. He replied that he had it on the impeccable authority of an eyewitness that we had practised on the course on the day of a competition in breach of Rule 7-1. I was so dumbstruck that he was able to scuttle away before I had a chance to explain his imbecilic misunderstanding prior to wringing his scrawny neck.

So we have no alternative, Mr Chairman, but to lodge a formal appeal with you to rescind our disqualification under the powers vested in you by Rule 33-7 and by doing so expunge all stains on our characters since the Rules of Golf do not apply any punitive sanctions for practising on the *cors* on the day of competition. In the meantime I shall have a sharp word with Freddy Holme for shooting off his mouth about our musical venture within earshot of that poisonous prat of a secretary.

Yours faithfully,
Jas. Pontifex

8

I REMEMBER THE FACE BUT I DON'T RECALL THE BALL

Dear Chairman,

You will be aware of the habit prevalent among a certain class of member of teeing the ball right on the line defining the forward boundary of the teeing ground. It is clearly prompted by a desire, albeit subconscious perhaps, to take advantage of the last millimetre of length on the drive. You and I, alumni of the university of life if I may so designate us, not to mention former pupils of the school of hard knocks, have long since learned the lesson that striving for the longest possible drive, whether consciously or spurred on by the shouted orders of some primitive instinct lurking in the murky depths of the psyche, is a positive guarantee of lashing the ball deep into the woods.

For my own part I make it a rule to tee the ball well back in the teeing ground as a reminder not to press on the shot but to concentrate on an accurate projection into the area I have deemed to be my target for the day, based on the siting of the flagstick, the weather and the underfoot conditions, power being the handmaiden of precision in my book. Mr Culpeper, on the other hand, always lays into the ball with every fibre of his being in an attempt on the world long-drive record, hence his practice of teeing up on the limit of the teeing ground. He is also very fussy about the quality of the turf into which he will plunge his tee peg.

You may well question the rationale for monitoring the grass when the ball is to be elevated a good inch above it. Don't ask me.

On the occasion of the first round of the July knock-out he had the honour on the first tee and went into his usual routine of determining the front margin of the teeing ground and casting around for an inviting patch of turf. His eye alighted on a satisfactory sward of fine fescue and he jabbed his tee into the ground. I am sure ... well, at least let us give him the benefit of any vestige of doubt and say that he had no devious intent in mind, but the fact is that he teed his ball a good two inches ahead of the markers. He hit a very good drive, by his standards. Now two inches at the start of a 400-yard hole is neither here nor there although the amount of tolerance could well account for a full stroke at the nether end of the hole. As we both know all too well, I could have recalled that drive from outside the teeing ground. But the Rules give me discretion in the matter and I deemed it preferable for the sake of a companionable match not to apply the full sanction of the laws in this case.

Nevertheless, I further deemed it advisable, for his sake you understand, to remind him as discreetly and diplomatically as possible of his obligations to the time-honoured rules and customs of the royal and ancient game. I said nothing, mind you, but I made rather a show of teeing up my ball three inches ahead of the markers and driving off. In his satisfaction at having nailed his drive he had omitted to retrieve his tee peg and the sight of it, standing there an inch behind my own tee peg, surely comprised a mute but eloquent rebuke.

My message struck home. As we walked up the fairway I could see him, scanning the Rule Book and then snapping it shut with the air of a man whose mind has settled firmly on a certain course of action. Not a word was spoken by either party on the next tee where Culpeper teed up half a yard in front of the markers. Purely for the purpose of driving home the lesson, I walked forward and teed up at the back of the ladies' tee. Culpeper's face was a mask as we advanced up the fairway in total silence.

As it happened I won that hole, although the outcome could not be attributed to any shortening of the hole, and so on the third I teed my ball about forty yards up the fairway. Culpeper selected a spot almost a cricket pitch further ahead.

I know that when you have an hour or two to spare you will want me to regale you with every last detail of the progress of the match. But for the present purposes, assisting you in your official duties of trying to make some kind of sense of the Rules of Golf, you will want me to stick to my regular procedure of confining myself to the barest and most pertinent bones of the case. Suffice it then to say that the match continued in a logical progression, with both parties proceeding farther and farther forward to find satisfactory places to tee the ball. I cannot stress too strongly that at no time did Culpeper and I agree 'to exclude the operation of any Rule or waive any penalty incurred'. You will notice that I have quoted the precise wording of Rule 1-3 with its pompous insistence on a capital letter for every mention of the word Rule and the illiterate inclusion of the completely unnecessary word 'incurred'. I do not have to remind you that Decision 2-5/1 states: 'In match-play a player may disregard a breach of the Rules by his opponent provided there is no agreement between the players.'

You might be tempted to conclude that, even though no words were spoken nor gestures made, there might have been some tacit understanding between us which could possibly be construed as an unspoken agreement to exclude the operation of Rule 11, which requires competitors to tee up within the appointed teeing ground. I assure you that such was not the case. You will be familiar, of course, with the famous concordat of 1951 when the Rules of Golf Committees of the Royal and Ancient Golf Club of St Andrews and the United States Golf Association harmonised their disparate codes of golf law and resolved in future to act in concert in making any necessary adjustments to the unified Rules of Golf. You will also know that, in the United States of America, the anti-trust laws require that before a plaintiff, such as the makers of Ping golf clubs, for example, can sue the pants off the USGA for damaging its business with daft legislation, proof must be offered that the defendants had conspired with another party or parties. If it is duly proved that the defendants acted in cahoots with another party, such as might be the Royal and Ancient Golf Club, then the aforementioned plaintiff could safely hire a fleet of wheelbarrows to carry off mountains of hundred dollar bills in actual, exemplary and punitive damages.

So the USGA loses no opportunity to shout from the rooftops that its Rules of Golf Committee acts independently in extending or adjusting golf law with never the slightest hint of consultation or collusion with any other party or parties. We are assured that not by written, spoken or telepathic communication does the USGA confer with the R and A before making its quadrennial revision of the Rules. The fact that the R and A comes out simultaneously with the same revision of Rules, identical to the American version right down to the last dot and comma, is pure coincidence. Of course it is. You swallow that assurance without cavil. By the same token you have my solemn pledge that there was no agreement, written, spoken or psychic, between Culpeper and me to exclude the operation of a Rule of Golf.

As the round progressed the character of the match changed, from golf to something more akin to pitch and putt. By dint of teeing up on the fringe of the green of the 560-yard seventeenth and holing the putt for a gross albatross, nett one, I squared the match as we went to the last hole. The Rules of Golf neglect to specify whether to place or drop when putting a ball into play on the green when playing from outside the teeing ground. Out of consideration for the putting surface I elected to place a ball on the edge of the last green before putting it up to the very lip of the hole for a certain two and, as I felt sure, a guarantee of going to extra holes at the very least.

'... *and dropped his ball into the hole.*'

You can imagine my surprise, Mr Chairman, when Culpeper in his turn advanced on the green, walked up and removed the flagstick, and then dropped his ball into the hole.

'You are perfectly at liberty to recall my shot,' he said, 'and to cancel my stroke and require me to play again from within the stipulated teeing ground, old boy.'

I was too dumbfounded to speak and Culpeper picked his ball from the cup and announced: 'In that case I win the hole in zero strokes gross, or nett minus one stroke, and with it the match one up. In compliance with the traditional courtesies of golf I am required at this point to commiserate with your ill fortune in not receiving due reward for your excellent play, to thank you most sincerely for the game and a most enjoyable afternoon and to wish you good day.'

With that he stalked off and reported his victory to the Secretary. My query, Mr Chairman, does not concern the manner of his 'winning' the last hole because we both know of several different ways it is possible to win a hole without playing a stroke. The point on which I seek your expert arbitration is whether Culpeper can be said to have completed the stipulated round, as required under Rule 1, when he did not actually play any part of the eighteenth hole in the accepted sense of the word. There is, of course, a Decision confirming that the result must stand in the case where the players inadvertently missed out one hole but, try as I might, I cannot see how it can be applied to save my friend's bacon. There was nothing inadvertent about his non-play of the last hole. In anticipation of your favourable judgment I shall hold myself in readiness to take part in the next round.

Yours faithfully,
Jas. Pontifex

9

WE OURSELVES ARE THE LITTLE THINGS SENT TO TRY US

Dear Chairman,

You will have heard of the disturbance in the club last Tuesday. No doubt in your other capacities as a member of the House Committee and the Membership Committee you will be making an assessment of the damage to furniture and fittings in the men's bar and also judiciously weighing the import of certain remarks made to the President about where he could stick membership of this club. I omit the adjectives used on that unfortunate occasion in the interests of delicacy. The origin of those distressing words and actions lies in the Rules of Golf. It is therefore my duty to place the full facts before you for adjudication.

My good friend Culpeper and I arranged to play in the monthly medal together, on the grounds that a companionable atmosphere would be inducive to our playing well. While we were changing in the locker room I noticed that Culpeper was removing that cardboard arrangement which manufacturers staple to socks these days. The socks themselves, I must say, were impressive, if that is the word: lime green and puce, with representations of the golfer on the follow-through worked into the pattern.

Culpeper pulled on these striking items, held up one foot and remarked: 'Worth a stroke a hole I shouldn't wonder.'

That remark was spoken in jest but it proved to

be prophetic. Culpeper was absolutely inspired on the course. I have never seen him hit the ball so well or so consistently. My own chances of getting among the silverware vanished, as per usual, in the watery depths of the pond at the third so I resolved to devote my energies to helping my friend make the most of his exceptional form. By this I mean to encourage and to keep his spirits up; nothing which in any way could be interpreted as outside advice or assistance in breach of Rule 8, you understand.

Thinking that a pair of Culpeper's socks might make a suitable Christmas present for one of my less refined friends, I had retrieved that cardboard wrapper from the waste basket in the locker room in order that I should have the name and address of the makers. During a lull in the proceedings on the course, when Culpeper departed into the shrubbery briefly in order, as we navy men put it, to shed a tear for Nelson, I read the sock manufacturer's blurb with a mounting sense of apprehension. This is what it said:

KUSH'N SOLE SOX. Guaranteed to put ten yards on your drive. Float on air like an astronaut with the miracle, space-age technology of Polypsychobabble, the wonder material which traps minute bubbles of air in the durable, odour-resistant soles of your KUSH'N SOLE SOX. You are guaranteed to add ten yards to every shot because you hit right through the ball, thanks to the assistance in the weight shift imparted by the magic of KUSH'N SOLE SOX.

You can probably imagine my feelings as the full import of those words sank in. My mind raced back to the San Diego Open of 1987 when Craig Stadler fell foul of Rule 13-3. As you know, Mr Stadler is a man of fastidious dress habits, in keeping with his trim build and neat appearance.

On the occasion in question his ball finished under a bush. Of necessity he had to kneel down to play it and he took the obvious precaution of laying a towel on the ground so that the knees of his designer

'I read the manufacturer's blurb with a mounting sense of apprehension.'

slacks should not become soiled. As an inevitable consequence of his dastardly action in thus 'building a stance' he was strung up by his thumbs for three days and beaten unmercifully with S-shafts by relays of the Rules of Golf committeemen.

Another example comes to mind. Wasn't the American pro John Huston warned that a pair of Weight-Rite golf shoes with built-in inserts to assist balance did not conform to the Rules of Golf? It is not really pertinent whether the Committee considered these shoes to be artificial aids or deemed them to constitute building a stance. The point is they were unlawful. So he bought a pair of normal golf shoes in the pro's shop and then went out and won the Honda tournament. And, if I may say so, you could not find a more inspiring example of how it pays to observe in both word and spirit all the Rules of Golf, even those which have clearly been thought up by dangerous madmen during a full moon.

I admit, Chairman, that I had to wrestle with my conscience. Loyalty to one's friends is a civilised duty, even unto death as we have so often seen during our turbulent island history. I give you Oates, the Scots Quaker, as just one example.

No one can predict how he will react in any given crisis but I like to think I would not be found wanting in defence of my good friend if Culpeper fell into a situation of physical danger or threat. On the other hand, unless the Rules of Golf are observed and upheld in every last detail, not just the sensible laws but every single one of them, the game is unplayable.

We golfers have to be our own policemen, judges and juries. And every once in a while the judge within us must steel himself to don the black cap and pronounce sentence of golfing death, even though the victim may be so close as to be almost one of the family. Taking the larger view, as we must, we recognise that justice actually benefits the prisoner at the bar more than it punishes him; insomuch as it sustains the game he loves and improves his knowledge of the laws. The sheer humanity of that reflection persuaded me as to my course of action.

By the time we were back in the locker room I knew where my duty lay. Culpeper came in bearing a bottle of champagne and two glasses.

'Career round warrants a small celebration, don't you think, me old mate? A 72 wouldn't mean anything to some people but for me it represents heaven on earth.'

He handed me his card.

'Here, stick your monicker on that. And by the way, thanks. Without your support and encouragement I don't think I could have done it.'

I do not know if you have ever tried to put the cork back into a bottle of champagne, Mr Chairman. That was Culpeper's first reaction when it got through to him that my refusal to sign his card was not some kind of leg-pull. I explained as best I could that his actual score was 216 once he had been assessed the two-stroke penalties due on each stroke for building a stance, or possibly using an artificial aid. I then cautioned him that you might make it 360 by penalising each foot separately for building twin stances.

'But look on the bright side,' I said. 'You have had the enjoyment of your round. And if I'd allowed that card to be submitted you would have suffered the ignominy of being disqualified for signing for a score lower than it should have been.'

It was this last remark which seemed to trigger the events which followed. I do hope, Chairman, that you will be able to resolve this matter in such a way that the friendship I have enjoyed with Culpeper for so many years will not be permanently impaired. I am sure that if you explain the situation to him with your usual diplomatic skill he will understand that I only did what was best for both of us and for the game of golf.

Yours faithfully,
Jas. Pontifex

10

NEAREST TO THE FLAG BUT FARTHEST FROM THE HOLE

Dear Chairman,

I do apologise for troubling you again but there seems to be no end to the possibilities for falling foul of the Rules of Golf and Mr Culpeper and I landed ourselves in another pretty pickle in the round robin. By way of background briefing I should explain that, while I am by far and away the superior striker and stylist, Culpeper's rather agricultural method can produce effective results at times and we are evenly matched when it comes to length off the tee.

This parity of power led us to devise a stimulating supplement to the usual run of greenies, sandies, golden ferrets and the host of other side bets with which golfers commonly spice their games. We call our novel invention Penny-a-yard. As the name implies it is in effect a long-driving competition on every tee, except for the par-threes. You may be interested to learn, incidentally, that it is very rare for more than twenty pence to change hands at the end of the day.

Quite apart from the added interest it brings to our golf, our Penny-a-yard wheeze makes us better and more considerate golfers. I think it is true to say that no one in the club is as meticulous in observing the conventions of the honour as Culpeper and me. It can be, and often is, argued that it makes not a blind bit of practical difference who takes the honour but I could never subscribe to such an iconoclastic notion. The honour is a survivor from the original thirteen Rules of Golf and it is incumbent upon us all to observe and respect all the Rules with equal diligence. The honour also represents a traditional courtesy from a more gracious and chivalrous age and deserves to be cherished for that reason alone.

We were all square coming to the last and so both of us were keyed up to hit our Sunday Specials. As you know, it seldom pays to put that extra bit of oomph into your drive. Culpeper hooked his into that enormous area of Ground Under Repair which is being re-turfed, and mine finished on the fairway, just, but in a puddle.

When we got up to our balls Culpeper called across the fairway: 'Got you by tuppence.' Sizing up the situation *vis-à-vis* our respective relief options, I replied: 'Don't count your chickens before they're hatched.'

I was required to drop my ball sideways onto the fairway but Culpeper's nearest point of relief was a good twelve yards back towards the tee.

'Far from being tuppence to you,' I remarked, 'methinks I shall be in pocket by about ten pence.' I deliberately adopted a jocular tone for this thrust because we had never formally adopted the appropriate Rule of Golf into the regulations for Penny-a-yard.

At this juncture Culpeper suffered what I presumed from his facial spasm to be a sharpish twinge of indigestion – that being the only logical explanation for what might easily have been mistaken for a deliberate expression of loathing and contempt, an unthinkable notion.

With ill grace he walked back and dropped his ball clear of the GUR. To my astonishment he now whipped out his three-iron, stepped up to his ball and hit an absolute ripper. It pitched about six feet from the stick, took two hops and stopped about three inches from the cup. He gave a whoop of delight and shouted: 'How do like dem apples, my fine bucko?'

Quick as a flash I made my riposte: 'Just be sure dem apples don't turn into sour grapes. It is with a heavy heart that I must recall that superb shot and require you to replay your stroke in the correct order of play.'

The ferocity, not to say vulgarity, of Culpeper's response caught me unawares. I must perforce censor and paraphrase a diatribe of extreme obscenity and profanity that constituted a totally unwarranted attack on my character. The gist must suffice, to the effect that his ball was clearly the further from the hole, as I had acknowledged by my squalid claim to have won ten pence, hence he had the honour, hence his shot was entirely valid, hence I might as well concede the hole and the match there and then, and further hence this time he was not going to fall for one of my devious attempts to pull a diabolical stroke of locker-room lawyerism.

I took all this with my usual stoicism, took out my volume of Decisions on the Rules of Golf and pointed out the relevant entry, Decision 10/1, which clearly states: 'The order of play is determined by the relative positions of the balls before relief is taken.' While Culpeper was digesting the import of this ruling, getting more and more agitated by the second, I played my shot, a poor one as it happened, into a greenside bunker.

Culpeper was still incandescent with rage as he snatched a ball from his bag, dropped it and made the most fearsome lunge at it with his three-iron. I don't know if you are familiar with Patrick Campbell's account of his boyhood golf in Cork when he played with a peppery character known as the Major. 'The head of the club buried itself in the mud nearly a yard behind the ball and remained there, leaving the shaft standing upright like a flagstick. It was not attended by the Major. The force of the impact had torn it from his hands.'

That is almost exactly how it happened with Culpeper. He stood like a statue for what I estimate to have been a full minute, holding the pose at the top of his follow through, breathing deeply and clenching and unclenching his empty hands. Then the tension in

'... breathing deeply and clenching and unclenching
his empty hands.'

his body dissolved and he went as limp as a rag doll. He retrieved the club, scraped the mud off its face with his shoe, made two languid swings and hit a beauty, right at the flag, which left him a six-footer for a four, as he called it.

He holed it after I had made a complete nonsense of the bunker job for a score of seven. Culpeper gave me a marked look and stalked off without saying a word, smug satisfaction oozing from every pore. He entered his name on the sheet as the winner by one up.

As you have no doubt surmised, the reason for my ludicrous thrashing about with the sand-iron was because my mind was in turmoil. I did not have the heart … No. I must be honest with myself and with you. I funked it. I was afraid for my physical safety with Culpeper in this volatile mood and so I did not say anything about the legality of his dropping a new ball when he already had a ball in play on the green. Or is a ball which has been played out of turn and recalled out of play? If so, is this the ball which must be put back into the play? The point is moot but I strongly suspect it is. Did he play a wrong ball? I await your ruling with interest and trust that you can see yourself clear to disqualify Culpeper and put yours truly through to the next round.

Yours faithfully,
Jas. Pontifex

11

ABSOLUTELY GUARANTEED: AN EXTRA 11.3 YARDS

Dear Chair,

I trust you will not deem this appellation as being unduly familiar. I have presumed to address you thus in the light of your recent response to my latest missive, which, as I observed, was headed: 'From the desk of the chair'. A sudden thought! Should I have addressed this note to 'Dear Desk'? My own office furniture being singularly illiterate I shall follow my usual routine of writing in person.

We all know that advertisers make ludicrously exaggerated claims for their products and if we took those claims at face value most golf equipment would not conform to the Rules of Golf. Hype and hogwash never added an inch to anybody's drive. But when you have the signed testimony of the Director of the Sports Science Research Centre of New York University, as subscribed and sworn to by Walter I. Schwartz, Notary Public, State of New York No. 01SC4756145, then you surely have to accept the claim as kosher and take it seriously, *vis-à-vis* the Rules of Golf.

My attention was called to a certain product during a friendly game with Mr Culpeper and I wish to make it crystal clear right from the start that in writing to you on this matter I am not asking for an adjudication on this particular round of golf. Far be it for me to drop Culpeper in it for an infringement, if such be the case, in a social round of golf between two friends.

Such pedantry is not beyond some people I could mention, and not a million miles from this very golf club, but nobody could ever accuse me of being one of those trouble-making locker-room lawyers.

I wasn't really paying much attention as Culpeper teed up on the first tee. He hit a decent enough drive, by his standards, and he gave me a smug look, like a cat which has just noticed that the catch on the canary's cage is not properly secured. Then I saw it. The object upon which he had teed his ball had not flown onto the ladies' tee as it usually does with him, nor had it flipped backwards the way it does for the pros and, if I may be so immodest as to mention it, for yours truly when I catch one off the screws. It had merely tilted forward and sat there, still stuck into the turf and leaning at a phallic angle. The object, made of white plastic, was twice the size of a normal tee peg, with a triangular top for the ball to sit on and the stem, instead of being circular in section, was shaped like a stubby knife blade.

'What in the name of all the saints and the lord of Zebedee is that thing?' I asked.

Culpeper gleefully responded: 'That, my old cock-a-doodlum, is Bob Gamble's Blast Off golf tee, patent pending.'

'But what does it do?'

'It would be quicker to recite what it doesn't do,' said Culpeper, drawing from his pocket the cardboard advertising material to which the tee had been attached. 'I quote: "Better directional control ... won't litter ... floats ... only tee to green tool ... best greens repair tool ... grooves, spikes and soles cleaner ... feels good to touch ... lucky stone ... could easily become your best golfing friend, dog's cock." '

'I only asked. There is no need for calling me vulgar names.'

'No,' said Culpeper, 'dog's cock is a term used in the printing industry to designate an exclamation mark.'

'But how does it help you play golf?' I persisted.

Culpeper read from another section of the blurb: ' "New York University's Physics Department 1989 tests prove unequivocally that balls hit from the Blast Off tee

'That ... is Bob Gamble's Blast Off tee, patent
pending.'

go dramatically farther than balls hit from wooden tees, three dogs' docks." '

He held up the card and pointed out the crimson headline that screamed: 'Hit Your Ball up to 11.3 yards MORE.'

Frankly, Mr Chairman, at this point I still entertained serious doubts about the Blast Off tee and sought to put it to critical examination.

'That drive you just hit. From your experience and the feeling imparted to your hands at impact, how far do you think you would have driven the ball of a regular, wooden tee?'

'That's easy,' said Culpeper. 'That was my 200-yard shot.'

'Let us see what advantage you have gained, if any, by using your patent pending tee.'

We both paced off the distance and both reached identical findings: 207 yards and 18 inches. Culpeper consulted a chart on the cardboard packaging. 'Two hundred yards converts to 207.5 yards. If you normally drive 300 yards, on the other hand, you would gain an extra 11.3 yards.'

It so happens that when I flush my six-iron I carry the ball exactly 150 yards in still air. In the interests of scientific enquiry I hit my six-iron on the next tee and caught it absolutely on the button. We paced off my shot at 155 and a half yards.

'A one fifty yards shot off a Blast Off tee goes 155.7 yards,' read Culpeper from the chart.

I felt slightly guilty at ever having doubted the veracity of this wonder tee's claims and asked what it cost.

Culpeper consulted the card. 'Six dollars and more than worth it, three dogs' cocks. But think of the saving. Listen to this: "Twenty-three million American golfers who buy one and a half to two billion tees annually will welcome this history-shattering tee because they can hit the ball farther and its virtual indestructability saves them money ... two thousand holes for one tee and three dogs' cocks." '

I felt sure that such a magical device must offend

against the provisions of Rule 14 as an artificial aid, but Culpeper pointed out the reassuring note: 'USGA accepted for play'. Well, they would, wouldn't they. After all the United States Golf Association's fortunes have been dissipated in expensive litigation trying to outlaw golf balls invested with the powers of perpetual motion and clubs which may or may not deviate from the approved form by half the thickness of a human hair. Financial distress has put the wind up the USGA and these days anything goes as far as they are concerned. A six-foot putter which you anchor by sticking the grip up the left nostril? Perfectly OK. Conforms in every respect with the definition of traditional form and make.

If the manufacturer of, say, cigar boxes advertised and marketed them as being made of finest wood and they turned out to be base metal then the President and CEO would be jumped on by the Better Business Bureau, the Advertising Standards Authority, the Cedar Wood Growers Association and the District Attorney. In the preamble to the Rules of Golf the USGA stresses that every word means what it says, except that 'wood' in the USGA dictionary embraces metal, plastic and ceramics, just as when they say that the referee's decision is 'final' they actually mean 'optional'.

But then I reflected that these days the lead of the USGA, petrified as it is by the threat of anti-trust laws, is not always followed by the Royal and Ancient Golf Club of St Andrews, which has dominion over the rest of the world of golf. It was inconceivable to me that the R and A could have approved such an obvious aid to better golf. I would ask them myself but the Rules of Golf Committee does not accept enquiries from individuals, only those from official bodies such as golf clubs. I really think we should establish the legality of this boon for golfers and, if necessary, post a list of Approved Tee Pegs on the notice board.

Yours faithfully,
Jas. Pontifex

12

DON'T BEND OR BREAK ME; I'M FIXED AND GROWING

Dear Chairman,

I don't know about you but I have always had a problem in the matter of instructing opponents and fellow competitors in the finer points of golf law. I mean, nobody could ever accuse me of lacking diplomatic tact but I can never forget a most unsavoury incident during our inaugural, and never-to-be-repeated, thank goodness, match against the local 'muni'.

I was drawn against a fellow with a florid tattoo on his forearm and a motley bag of clubs, not one of which bore any family relationship to the others. As you well know there is not an ounce of snobbery in my body and I was quite prepared to accept him as a diamond in the raw. And he certainly gave the ball a healthy crunch with his untutored action. I had a real job staying in the match, I can tell you, and my prospects were looking bleak by the thirteenth hole.

That was where his bucolic swing betrayed him and his drive landed among those bushes on the right. His ball lay in the clear but beside a bush in such position that he had no stance and, even if he had, the branches would have impeded the swing path of his club. To my dismayed amazement he took his wedge and absolutely demolished that bush with what he deemed to be practice swings. Despite the worthy

'... took his wedge and absolutely demolished that bush with practice swings.'

purpose of the match, namely to extend hands across the social barrier, I had perforce to intervene.

'My dear old chap,' I said, 'you have not had my advantages of education and instruction in the finer points of this noble and honourable game and due allowances must be made for your humble, though doubtless honest, background, no aspersions on those grounds, you understand. But you will forgive me if I explain that the rules actually state: "A player shall not improve his lie by moving, bending or breaking anything growing or fixed except in fairly taking his stance."'

He turned ugly. I thought for a moment the ruffian was going to visit physical violence upon my person. He yelled: 'Are you calling me a cheat, squire?'

Naturally, I demurred, but he was not to be placated.

'Don't you come the great "I am" with me, you toffee-nosed merchant banker,' he snarled.

I was quite taken aback by this lapse into the vernacular and forebore to assure him that I had never worked in a bank. He continued his verbal assault, bunching his fist in my face and shouting: 'Anybody calls me a cheat gets one right up the hooter.'

I backed away, remarking: 'Shall we continue with the game?' It was a lame response, Mr Chairman, and as some might think a cowardly one, but frankly I had no idea how to combat such raw yobbism. I was shaking and sweating and my mind was in a turmoil. Obviously enough, I could not hit my hat but that dreadful oik was completely unaffected by the incident and polished me off with aplomb.

My experience was not unique. Many others have told me their games have gone completely to pot after attempting, in all good faith, to instruct a fellow competitor in a correct procedure. One learns and, unless one has the moral fibre of a John Knox, like Bernard Gallacher, one develops diplomatic blindness at minor infringements.

Mr Culpeper is nothing if not a perfect gentleman and takes my gentle admonitions on golf law in the spirit in which they are offered. In most cases, that is. But there are times when the inconsistencies and vagaries of the Rules try him sorely and he is moved to make forceful comments on them. Such was the case this morning when he felt he had been victimised by a legal caprice. It is for this reason that I am seeking endorsement of my interpretation of the laws so that Culpeper will be reassured that I was not seeking personal advantage from the situation.

We were all square on the last tee and Culpeper went for a big one in order to swing the match his way. As always, when he tries to belt the ball into the next time zone he made a hash of things. The sole plate of his driver grazed the top of his ball and sent it scuttling onto the ladies' tee. I hit a steady one which tailed off in the high rough on the left.

He took his three-wood and hit his second shot into what seemed to be the identical spot. Seeking to give him a subtle reminder about the approved procedure when searching for a ball I remarked: 'Have you got your wrist watch on, old boy? Save me getting mine out of the bag.' That proved to be a timely – no pun intended, Chairman – intervention because after a lapse of four minutes and fifteen seconds we had not found either ball. 'Nothing else for it,' said Culpeper, and we retraced our steps for the stroke-and-distance routine. He dropped his ball and I teed up.

At this point there was a shout from up the fairway. That new greenkeeper, nice chap, Hogbottom or some such name, had just started gang-mowing that rough, and not before time if you ask me. He climbed down from the tractor, bent down and then shouted 'Titleist one and Topflight six.' Culpeper glanced at his watch and announced: 'Just in the nick of time.' I shook my head, investing that action with as much sympathy as I could register.

'Afraid not. You have dropped another ball and under the Rules of Golf that is now the ball in play. Your first ball which was lost and has just been found is deemed to be lost.'

He pondered that intelligence for a moment and then said: 'Well get on with it, then. You're away.'

'No, no,' I replied, picking up my ball and tee peg, 'It is your honour, my dear chap.'

'What on earth do you think you are doing?' asked Culpeper, 'You have just picked up your ball in play. Unless I am very much mistaken that means a penalty stroke.'

I disabused him as gently as possible. 'No. Since I had to play from the teeing ground I was permitted to put my ball on a tee peg. That action in itself did not constitute putting a ball into play. The replacement or substitute ball does not become the ball in play until I make a stroke at it. Now the definition of a stroke ...'

He interrupted me with a howl of anguish. 'You're at it again, you swine. You are bamboozling me with rulesmanship.' I asured him that no bam had been boozled; I was simply following the correct procedure.

You can imagine the rest. He made a thorough hash of his next shot and, thanks to the passage of the gang-mower, my ball was sitting up in an excellent lie. I hit it onto the green with a swing of careless rapture and in due course trousered the booty which was handed over, I might add, with bad grace and obvious reluctance. I shall be most obliged, Mr Chairman, to have reassurance for Culpeper that he was not conned out of the match.

Yours faithfully,
Jas. Pontifex

P.S. We are assured by the Rules of Golf that a player is entitled to the lie his shot gave him, meaning that if he drives on the fairway and a passing tractor then squashes it waist deep into the mud then the player may restore his original lie. I would just like to stress, Mr Chairman, that there is nothing in the rules, absolutely nothing, which says that if a gang-mower improves the lie that your shot gave you that you should lift and drop your ball in the nearest patch of equivalent rough.

13

DOES MY BONNY LIE OVER THE LATERAL WATER HAZARD?

Dear Chairman,

George Bernard Shaw contended that all the learned professions were confidence tricks against the public. He based this proposition on the predilection of professional bodies for inventing their own jargon that nobody could understand, hence creating unlimited scope for charging exorbitant fees for unscrambling the incomprehensible. Sociology is a good case in point since this scientific discipline consists of setting up complex and expensive experiments to discover what anyone with an ounce of common sense knows already. Psychology is roughly similar, obscuring the obvious behind a smokescreen of psychobabble. Medicine is a frightful fraud, with its coded language, such as 'I'd like to call in another opinion on this', which translates as: 'I haven't the slightest idea what that lump is but if I refer you to Freddy I can be sure he will split his fee with me.' But with all due respect for your own distinguished career, Mr Chairman, and your unrivalled reputation at the bar in your specialised field of defending child molesters, I have to say that the worst profession of all for bamboozling the public is the law. The law speaks in archaic English spattered with Latin aphorisms and 'whereases' and 'heretofores' and 'parties of the third part' and is, in its written form, devoid of all punctuation.

Since the Rules of Golf Committees are traditionally loaded down to the Plimsoll line with lawyers, it is hardly surprising that the Rules are immensely complicated and written in legal gobbledygook which the poor layman cannot understand let alone remember. As for lumbering us with two codes of rules, for match-play and stroke-play, with different scales of penalty for identical infringements, I cannot help but feel a certain sympathy for those who believe that the Rules of Golf represent not only a conspiracy against us golfers but also a betrayal of the game's heritage, which they purport to maintain.

These uncharacteristically sombre reflections arise from a recent visit to the United States with Mr Culpeper. We pondered long and hard before deciding on this vacation venue but Squiffy Rogers, who runs a bucket-shop in Whitechapel when he isn't chairing the House Committee, came up with a couple of cheap if slightly iffy tickets to LA, so off we went. We based ourselves at Monterey so that we would be handy for the courses along Seventeen Mile Drive. Our choice was influenced by a terrific slice of luck. Culpeper found a man's wallet on the floor of the boot-splasher on the flight over and after he handed it in to a stewardess the owner came over to thank him. We got to talking and when we told him our plans he said if there was anything he could do for us to just say the word. Bold as brass Culpeper said: 'You couldn't get us on to Cypress Point, could you?' Blow me if this chap didn't turn out to be a member and said he would be delighted to host us.Terrific course but that famous sixteenth is a phoney. It is as obvious as the nose on your face that Alistair MacKenzie designed it as a short par-four and you can even see the traces of the original tee among the cypresses on the bank. As a par-three it is ridiculous for ordinary mortals. Culpeper lost six balls in the ocean and I lost seven.

We had reluctantly decided to give Pebble Beach a miss because of the exorbitant expense of the green fee and the compulsory cart and all that. It costs an arm and a leg. But our freebie at Cypress Point had put us ahead of the game so we said, 'What the hell, what's an arm and a leg among friends?' The beauty of the place inspired us to play our best golf, both of us level par through the turn which isn't bad for a couple of fiscal amputees. The day turned sour on us at the par-three seventeenth. You know the one, where Tom Watson did his war dance after chipping in from the clag. We had a brisk wind coming straight at us and that meant taking the heaviest furniture off the tee. Culpeper's drive paid off in the wind and landed in a shallow drainage ditch running with a healthy trickle of water from the overnight storm. It subsequently transpired that this stream carried Culpeper's ball onto the beach, close to the high-water mark. I tacked forward against the wind and got my third fairly close to the flagstick. At that point I saw Culpeper preparing to take a drop and just managed to arrest him in this rash procedure with my warning shout.

'Listen, old chap,' I said when I reached the scene, 'you have a very good score going on one of the greatest championship courses in the world. I could never forgive myself if I allowed you to incur unnecessary penalty strokes through following a wrong procedure. Be guided by someone who has made a lifetime study of the Rules of Golf.'

He gave me a wary look and replied in controlled monotone: 'A water hazard is defined as "any sea, lake, pond, river, ditch, surface drainage ditch or other open water course (whether or not containing water) and anything of a similar nature". Note particularly the prominence given in that Definition to the sea. This is a sea, specifically the Pacific Ocean. It is designated in the local rules as a lateral water hazard. Furthermore its margin is delineated by red posts. I propose to take relief from this lateral water hazard under the procedure prescribed by Rule 26. Now piss off and stop trying to ruin my holiday for me.'

What could I do, Mr Chairman? I held my peace. I would certainly not begrudge handing over a dollar wager to a good friend to whom I would gladly give the shirt off my very back. A minor technical infringement should not be allowed to come between friends, don't

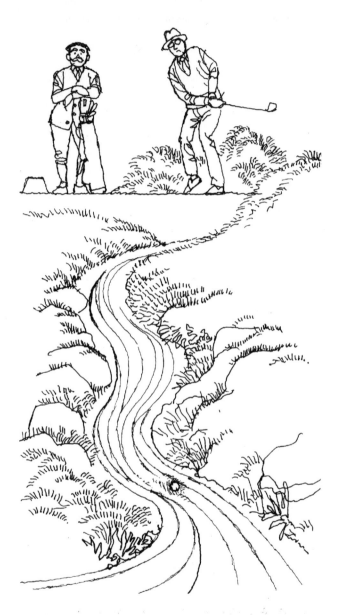

'... this stream carried Culpeper's ball onto the beach.'

you agree? But in submitting his card for handicap adjustment we are entering the realm of personal integrity and meticulous accounting procedures. There can be no room for sentiment. So stern duty requires me to draw your attention to Decision 26-1/7 which makes it clear that any extension of a water hazard which lies outside the boundary of the course is not part of the hazard but out of bounds. This Decision is fairly recent so I will not castigate the United States Golf Association for wrongly defining the Pacific Ocean as a lateral water hazard in half a dozen US Open Championships. Nor will I dwell over long on the anomaly of a Definition specifying any sea as a water hazard and a Decision deeming it to be out of bounds. I will confine myself, and that with a heavy heart, to pointing out that when a flow of water carries a ball beyond the boundary of the course the correct procedure is to follow the dictates of Rule 27-1; that is, in this instance, to go back and play three off the tee.

Yours faithfully,
Jas. Pontifex

14

A RARE CASE OF THE FAN HITTING THE WHAT?

Dear Chairman,

I must say that since Mr Culpeper has been playing with and against me on a regular basis he has made a real effort to master the Rules of Golf, and all credit to him. But that old cove Alexander Pope hit the nail on the whatsit when he wrote that 'A little learning is a dangerous thing', and I must draw your attention to the incident which compelled me to complete the couplet for Culpeper's benefit: 'Drink deep', I so admonished him, 'or taste not the Pierian spring.'

Forgive me, for I am getting ahead of myself. Not like me, that. As you know, I usually get straight to the point and confine myself strictly to the bare facts. Which is precisely what I shall now do. We were playing the short par-five and for only the second time in my entire life I was on the green in two, albeit on the far edge a long way from the flagstick. In the interests of speeding up the pace of play, as so exhorted in many a notice penned by your good self, I hurried directly to the green since Culpeper was on the other side of the fairway and could in no way be inconvenienced by my walking forward. He lay some sixty yards short of the green in two and I waited with putter poised to watch his shot.

(On that subject, Mr Chairman, I am distressed that a growing number of golfers, and some of them our own club members, to our shame, do not extend to opponents the courtesy of watching the destiny of their shots. They are therefore unable to assist in locating a ball which may have landed in woods or sedge. That is not how I was brought up to behave on the golf course, and you neither, I'll be bound. In the winter knock-out I had occasion to play against one of the former artisan members whom the Council in its wisdom – a figure of speech, that, and not the *mot juste* I would necessarily have selected – granted full membership. I hit one off the toe and since I tend to keep my eye on the spot from which the ball has departed, as instructed by all the teaching manuals, I was obliged to ask my horny-handed adversary if he had noted the destination of my shot. He replied gruffly: 'Find your own ball.' I omit the obligatory adjective appended willy nilly on every conceivable occasion by this class of fellow, singularly inappropriate in this case since it ascribed to a golf ball a function of which it is clearly incapable.)

As I was saying, I watched Culpeper's shot and, since it was headed for the opposite edge of the green, I deemed it the appropriate moment to hit my putt. Which I duly did. At that moment an extraordinary apparition sprang from the bushes. It was an elderly party with a wispy ginger beard. He wore corduroy trousers and open-toed sandals and a thing like a caddie jacket emblazoned with the legend: 'CAMPAIGN AGAINST GOLF.' Shouting, 'You swine are defiling the environment and destroying the habitats of God's dumb creatures!' he snatched up both our golf balls as they rolled across the verdant turf and hurled them into the lake.

With a sprightly leap which belied his advanced years, he then disappeared into the undergrowth, affording me no opportunity to inform him that our course had been a rat-infested slag-heap which had been landscaped into a magnificent championship layout and subsequently colonised by a huge variety of birds, insects and mammals including rabbits, hares, foxes, grey squirrels, frogs, toads, newts and badgers. I would, if I could, have further advised him of the three

71

'It was an elderly party with a wispy ginger beard.'

varieties of orchid which have required the rough to the left of the fourteenth to be designated a Site of Special Scientific Interest. Probably wouldn't have done any good, anyway. He looked like the type who gets his jollies out of protesting and waving banners about and does not much care what cause he supports.

Culpeper had him tagged correctly as an outside agency and opined that since we could not play our deflected balls as they lay, we should replay both strokes under Equity. I perforce had to demur. Certainly I must replay my stroke (Decision 19-1/4), a procedure which suited my books, not that this was a consideration in making my legal judgment, since my putt had not been a good one. But as for Culpeper, I recalled a precedent from the presumptuously designated World Match-play Championship. (How can a cigarette company promote a championship? Championship of what? Inhaling carcinogens?) You probably remember the incident on the sixteenth hole where Nick Faldo drove into the trees on the left in his match against Graham Marsh. He, Faldo that is, played a wonderful shot which curled around the trees onto the line to the green, although he could not see it from where he was in the woods. The ball came in hot, as the pros say, and flew right across the green.

A drunken spectator was standing at the foot of the bank behind the green and as Faldo's ball bounded towards him he deftly volleyed it with his right foot back onto the green. It stopped a yard from the hole. The sober members of the gallery were outraged and there was a vociferous consensus that sportsmanship demanded Faldo offer Marsh a half. The referee asked a marshal whether the ball had been in motion when it was deflected and, on being assured that such was the case, he told Faldo to play his ball as it lay.

Faldo, who had seen and knew nothing of what had occurred, played to the referee's figurative whistle. Such was the public resentment at this blatant breach of natural justice that one spectator grabbed Faldo by the throat and called him a cheating bastard. One of those journalist chappies wrote in his newspaper that this was a rare case of the fan hitting the shit. That was most unfair since Faldo was an innocent party who had done no more than obey the referee's instruction.

Such was the furore raised by the incident that the chief referee was consulted and, as I believe, he in turn consulted the authorities at the Royal and Ancient Golf Club at St Andrews before issuing a statement that the original decision must stand but that in cases of deliberate interference by a spectator the referee should put the ball in the place that he deemed would have been its final resting place, if undeflected, from the original shot.

Accordingly, Mr Chairman, I informed Culpeper that I must cancel my putt, replace a ball and have another go. But a different procedure was involved in the case of a ball played from off the green and deliberately deflected by a spectator. So saying, I asked Culpeper for a ball, which he gave me. I then rolled it across the green, it went down the bank and came to rest under a bush. He gave the appearance of a man who had been struck smartly behind the ear with a sock full of wet sand, mumbling incoherently 'What the ... ?'

He eventually cooled down after I had explained the *raison d'être* or rationale of my action. We played on but he was not himself. When I told him about that fan joke he enquired bitterly if there was anything in the Rules of Golf which empowered an opponent to hit the shit. So my purpose in appealing to you today, Mr Chairman, is to enquire whether you could see yourself clear to deduct a stroke a hole from Culpeper's scores for all the holes played after that traumatic and quite unprecedented incident. Deducting seven strokes would at least give him a total in double figures and save his face in some degree. Surely the doctrine of Equity could stretch a point in this case.

Yours faithfully,
Jas. Pontifex

15

MAN THE GOLFER, OR MAN THE OPEN-CAST MINER?

Dear Chairman,

The Rules of Golf are curiously ambiguous on the subject of when and how a ball may be declared unplayable. Oh, Rule 28 seems clear enough: 'The player may declare his ball unplayable at any place on the course except when the ball lies in or touches a water hazard. The player is the sole judge of whether his ball is unplayable.' Fair enough, on the face of it. But does this mean you can declare your ball unplayable when it is in your pocket? Common sense tells us that common sense would never contemplate such a procedure, but the question could arise. More likely is the question of whether a player can deem his ball unplayable when he does not know the location of such ball. And that is the subject of my enquiry today, because frankly I am flummoxed. As always when a question of interpretation comes up I go rummaging through the book of Decisions for enlightenment. The answer came up right off the bat with the very first Decision, Number 28/1: 'A player may proceed under the stroke and distance option without finding his ball.' But the very next Decision, 28/2 contains this admonition: '... he must find the original ball before he can declare it unplayable.' Clear as mud, what?

This subject came to a head in the monthly medal when Mr Culpeper's ball plugged under the lip of that absolute stinker of a bunker on the twelfth fairway. When I say 'plugged' I mean plugged. The ball had completely disappeared from sight and only a residual trickle of powdery sand gave us a clue as to its resting place. In my usual spirit of helpfulness, I warned Culpeper that he was permitted only to brush away enough sand or other loose impedimenta to establish the location of a golf ball. He was not permitted to clear away enough debris to identify the ball as his; but no matter, there was no penalty for playing a wrong ball in this situation. He could go on locating balls and playing them, without penalty, until he eventually played his own ball.

He was meticulous in brushing aside the sand, not quite grain by grain but with feather-light strokes with his fingers until at last he cried: 'Here's a ball!' I don't suppose it had penetrated three inches into the sand, more like buried three inches deep in a landslide of sand, but the result was the same. It was a dreadful lie, sunk deep under the projecting brow which was itself further extended by a mass of heather.

'Cut your losses, my old mate,' I cried, 'and declare it unplayable.'

'What, drop it within two clubs' lengths, not nearer the hole, and within the hazard?'

I had to disabuse him of any such procedural irregularity. 'No, you can't do that. Nor can you take it back and drop it in the bunker, keeping its location in line with the flagstick.'

'Why not?' he enquired with that hint of suspicion in his voice.

'Because both those options are dependent on the location of your ball and you do not know that this is your ball. You don't know for sure where your ball is.'

'I can soon find out by pulling that ball out and identifying it.'

'No that is exactly what you can't do. Rule 12 specifically forbids removing enough sand or loose impedimenta to identify a ball. Your only choice under the unplayable ball rule is stroke and distance.'

'Go back two hundred and twenty odd yards and

lose the advantage of my best drive of the day? Not on your nelly, old sport. I shall put my faith in Old Equaliser to get me out of this mess.'

So saying, he grabbed that monstrosity of a wedge from his bag and took an almighty smack at the ball. Sand and sundry specimens of local flora flew everywhere, blocking out the sun. Small mammals cowered with fear in their burrows. When the dust settled he resumed his careful scraping of sand from the bunker face until his sensitive fingers detected a ball. Where it had been about three inches under the lip it was now a good seven inches into the sand. Culpeper stood there surveying the scene of devastation: 'I guess you were right. There is nothing else for it but declare the damn thing unplayable.'

Painful though it was, I had to demur. 'As I have already explained, in this situation your only option under the unplayable ball rule is stroke and distance. Whereas taking your ball back to the site of the previous stroke was extremely cogent advice a minute ago before you started open-cast mining, taking your ball back to the site of your previous stroke now places the ball three inches into the sand. Just as bad if not worse than your present lie, wherever that may be.'

Culpeper gave me a look of purest hatred, as if to indicate that I was a party to some dire conspiracy to ruin his score and his day's pleasure. He then resumed excavation. Three savage blows created a furrow about eighteen inches long and almost as deep. He slumped, panting from his exertions. Then an idea put the backbone back into him. 'The limits of a hazard extend vertically upwards and downwards, do they not?'

I concurred with a nod and a frown.

'Ergo, the ball is now well outside the limits of the hazard. Ergo, I am no longer constrained by the regulations governing play within a hazard. Ergo, I am now a free man and sitting pretty, if that is the word, through the green. Ergo, I can now lift my ball to identify it. Ergo, I can deem it unplayable and drop it within two clubs' lengths not nearer the hole. With a one stroke penalty, of course.'

I hated to do it, Mr Chairman, but you and I know all too well that when a player goes in for this kind of wholesale landscaping and tunnels his way through the vertical limits of the hazard his ball is nevertheless deemed to be still within the hazard. I conveyed this intelligence to Culpeper with all the sympathy I could muster.

My words seemed to trigger some atavistic response deep within Culpeper's psyche. He went absolutely berserk, attacking Mother Earth with a fury which was frightening to behold. He rained blows with that wedge at such a furious pace that I could scarcely perform my due function as a marker of keeping count. On the twenty-seventh blow the ball popped up onto the turf. I think that this must have been the stroke that ripped the stitches of his recent hernia operation. Give him full marks for pluck. He completed the round, flapping at the ball with innocuous little hand and arm shots which popped the ball forward in a succession of twenty-yard hops. Between shots he walked doubled over and clutching his groin. Coming up the last, Colonel Rumbold snarled at him from the first green: 'For God's sake stop that groaning, man, while I'm trying to putt.'

Mr Chairman, I have searched the Rule Book and I have searched my conscience and I cannot fault the interpretations which I had to make on Culpeper's behalf. Perhaps you would be kind enough to reassure me on that point. But the essential question I have to put to you in your official capacity is whether the game of golf is intended to create wholesale damage to the course and to inflict physical pain on its adherents. All my life I have cherished the notion that one of the purposes of our beloved pastime was to promote good health and good fellowship.

'He went absolutely berserk, attacking Mother Earth with fury.'

P.S. I took the liberty in your absence of adding your name to the get well card we got up for Culpeper. When I took it round to the cottage hospital they called up to his ward and I was given the message to leave the card at the front office. He must be in a bad way indeed if they won't let him see his best friend.

Yours faithfully,
Jas. Pontifex

16

THE BEST DROPS IN LIFE ARE FREE

Dear Chairman,

We all understand perfectly well that the Rules of Golf are not just a series of prohibitions and punishments but that they also comprise the golfer's Bill of Rights. On those occasions when the Rules offer a favour then we can seize it with never a shadow falling on our reputations for sportsmanship. If the nearest point of relief from a puddle in the rough is on the fairway then we take advantage of our good fortune with never a twinge of guilt. The guardians of our morals on the Rules of Golf Committee do not give a hoot. Come to that they do not even distinguish between fairway and rough, lumping them both together under the heading of 'Through The Green'.

But in my humble opinion there comes a point where honour, personal probity and the unwritten moral standards of the game do come under challenge. That is when a player scrupulously adheres to the letter of the Rules but at the same time manipulates them to his advantage. This is a grey area, of course, but a chap from a decent home and a decent school knows instinctively where the line must be drawn between legitimate tactics, such as walking and playing swiftly when you know your opponent likes to dawdle, and an overt attempt to put your man off his stroke by deliberately whistling off-key when playing a music lover.

The point at issue is what action should be taken, if any, when that line is crossed. I well remember the example of the late Henry Cotton when acting as a referee during a tournament in Portugal. A contestant drove under a large tree with spreading branches drooping to ground level. The ball lay close to the trunk of the tree in such a position that the chap could not get a swing at it. However, the entire area under the canopy of that expansive tree was spotted with mole hills.The player addressed the ball and one foot was on a mole hill. He asked for and was granted a free drop, a tricky operation because this was in the days of dropping over the shoulder and it required considerable athleticism to perform these rites while bent over double under the branches. Not at all by accident, the ball dropped right by another mole hill. With Cotton's permission he repeated the process, not once but five more times. By a process of selective dropping the player was working his way towards a spot clear of the tree where he would have an unimpeded shot at the green. Cotton was a downy old bird who had seen it all a hundred times and knew from appearances that he was dealing with a human rodent, endowed with basic cunning but no profound knowledge of the Rules or anything else. He thus forbade a seventh drop, announcing sternly that the man's shot had given him a lie under the tree and that therefore he must play from under the tree. The poor blighter just had to scoot the ball out sideways. Bernard Shaw once observed that a small falsehood might well be permissible for the sake of a greater veracity and I suppose that a small deviation from the letter of the law is equally permissible for the sake of a greater justice.

You may be unaware that Mr Culpeper is completely ambidextrous. As a youth he won a competition playing right-handed in the morning and using a left-handed set for the second round in the afternoon. These days he habitually carries a left-handed seven-iron as part of his regular set and uses it whenever there are problems standing to the ball for a right-handed shot.

Yesterday we were playing in the winter knock-out and he cut his drive at the fourteenth way up into the rabbit warren among that mass of gorse bushes. You would be hard put to find a single square yard of ground that was not pitted with a rabbit scrape and when we found his ball sitting pretty out in the open he addressed it with that left-handed club and announced that his stance was impeded by a rabbit scrape. I asked him why he was using the left-handed club and he replied rather tartly that he was the sole judge of the shot he planned to play. I did not argue the point and he took his drop. Now he put back that seven iron and addressed the ball with his right-handed three iron. 'Oh dear,' he said. 'Blow me if my other foot isn't in a rabbit scrape this time.'

I will not bore you with all the details of subsequent drops or my interjections about his using that left-handed club to get advantageous drops. He simply kept repeating that he was the sole judge of how to play the shot. Suffice it to say that, finally, a drop from the left-handed club put him into the clear and he played his next onto the green with a right-handed club. I demurred, saying that he should have used the club with which he had obtained relief but he replied (quite correctly as it happens, because I looked it up later) that dropping the ball produced a completely new situation which had to be re-evaluated as to which club would be most appropriate.

In all he contrived to take ten free drops and, while I had this uneasy feeling that something was terribly wrong, I could not see any hint of a breach of proper golf procedure. I do not have the moral authority to impose my own notions of fair play on the situation like Henry Cotton, but then I am still not convinced that Cotton's solution had any validity in golf law.

Culpeper won the hole and it was by that margin of one hole that he won the match. Lord knows, nobody could ever accuse me of acting under the impulse of sour grapes. My only motive, as always, is to uphold the rule of golfing law in both letter and spirit. If, in consultation with higher authorities, you decide that the procedures in this case were not

'He addressed it with that left-handed club and announced that his stance was impeded ...'

entirely *comme il faut* and you decide that the result of this match must be reversed then you and I will have the satisfaction of knowing that our public spirited action has hooked another dead cat out of the pure well of golf law. It may well be in these peculiar circumstances that you will have great difficulty in reaching a firm decision one way or another. In that case I counsel the wise dictum which is common currency in the Inns of Court, namely: 'If in doubt find against the shit.'

Yours faithfully,

Jas. Pontifex

17

WHAT DO YOU THINK YOU ARE PLAYING AT?

Dear Chairman,

My regular golfing companion, Mr Culpeper, has made strenuous efforts since we started playing together to learn the Rules of Golf. When I recently congratulated him on his progress he replied in jest: 'Sheer self-defence, old boy.' He really is a card, that man.

However, you and I know all too well that there exists a gulf as wide as the Grand Canyon between a working knowledge of the basic, iron rations of golf and the mastery of the subtleties of golf law, especially the *esoterica* to be found in the small print of the game's case law, or Decisions. Naturally, I am anxious to instruct Mr Culpeper in what, as a keen amateur musician, I like to think of as the grace notes of golfing jurisprudence.

I have observed, as you may well have too, Mr Chairman, that there is a certain class of golfer who is quite unable to appreciate the beauty, the clarity, the elegance and the sheer scope of the written code. I have even heard some churlish fellows dismiss the rules as pseudo-legalistic gobbledygook, for goodness sake!

It therefore behoves those of us with the intellectual powers to absorb and appreciate the Rules with their attendant Definitions and Decisions to work patiently and diligently at our missionary work of instructing the ignorant. I am sure you will not misinterpret my motives when I tell you, Mr Chairman, that in my experience the sharp shock of a two-stroke penalty is a powerful teaching aid in getting the pupil to understand and remember a point of law. Never in a million years would I stoop to exploiting an opponent's ignorance of the Rules for my own personal advantage and in those cases where I am forced by stern duty to impose a penalty I do so in a spirit of honest endeavour to convert a heathen. I shall not labour the point further, but simply ask you to bear my words in mind in assessing the justice of the following incidents.

In the mid-week medal the other day Culpeper drove into that patch of fairway on the second where the green staff has been re-turfing. His ball lay in a crevice between two turfs – or should that be turves? I am never sure of those f-word plurals like whether it should be poofs or pooves – and it was a really horrid lie. Accordingly he declared his ball unplayable and lifted it. He then looked round and asked: 'What are those blue sticks?'

'Not sticks,' I corrected him, 'but stakes. If you had taken the elementary precaution of checking the notice board in the locker room you would have seen a note to the effect that this area has been temporarily designated as ground under repair and is marked as such by blue stakes.'

He flushed and had to begin his response all over again, the opening words gushing forth a full octave above his normal baritone. 'Do you mean to say that you stood idly by while I declared my ball unplayable, thus lumbering myself with a penalty stroke, when you knew all along that I was entitled to a free drop out of that scabby lie? You are pulling another one of your swifties, aren't you?'

My reply, while not particularly musical, certainly had powers to soothe the savage breast: 'In these circumstances the declaring or deeming of your ball to be unplayable and the subsequent lifting of same do not commit you irrevocably to proceed under Rule 28. Pray determine your nearest spot affording complete relief from the condition and drop the ball without penalty.'

You will notice, Mr Chairman, that on this

occasion it was the threat of a penalty, albeit a spurious threat generated within the suspicious mind of my adversary, that drove the message home.

I told Culpeper: 'Let this be a lesson to you.'

Instead of employing an appropriate tone of gratitude, he replied with a snarl: 'I won't forget this little lesson in a hurry.'

The rest of the match passed without further incident or, for that matter, conversation.

Yesterday we met in the mid-week knock-out and by coincidence Culpeper drove into that patch on the ninth where they are using up the spare turf, or turves, to repair the damage caused by leaking hydraulic fluid from the tractor. Once again, as it transpired, he had a beastly lie and again, as it further transpired, his ball proved to be in ground under repair.

My drive was not as long as his and so, in the interests of not delaying play, I perforce had to hit my shot before hurrying forward to give Culpeper the benefit of my knowledge and experience. Murphy's Law now intervened. Just when I wanted to get to the scene of Culpeper's ball with the utmost despatch my progress was interrupted by a loose shoelace. To my great distress, by the time I got there Culpeper had taken his free drop and played his shot.

'Funny thing, that,' he remarked, 'twice in one week declaring my ball unplayable and then discovering it was in GUR. Still, thanks to you and your timely lesson on the first occasion I knew exactly how to proceed this time.'

Have you ever wondered, Mr Chairman, how a doctor must feel when he has to deliver a fatal diagnosis? I don't know why, but for some reason I felt it might soften the blow if I addressed him by his first name, which happens to be Basil, although he would not like that to become public knowledge, for obvious reasons.

'Baz, old boy,' I said as gently and sympathetically as I could, 'this is match-play.'

'So what?' he responded belligerently, 'It is still golf. And don't call me Baz!'

'Once again he had a beastly lie.'

'Match-play is a different form of golf. Different rules apply. When you deemed your ball unplayable you incurred a penalty stroke. Right?'

'No I certainly did not! I discovered that my ball was in ground under repair so I took a free drop. All perfectly kosher and above board.'

'But you admit that you did declare your ball unplayable?'

'Yes, but I rescinded that declaration when I found out I was due a free drop.'

'Nonetheless, by making the declaration and picking up your ball you were, for those few moments, liable to a penalty stroke.'

'If you say so, clever Dick. What's the difference?'

'Rule 9-2 states: "A player who has incurred a penalty shall inform his opponent as soon as practicable." You did not inform me of any penalty. I had to drag it out of you. Let me continue with the Rule: "If he fails to do so, he shall be deemed to have given wrong information…" '

Culpeper howled: 'But I did not know I had incurred a penalty. How could I tell you something I did not know?'

'Permit me to finish the Rule,' I replied in a flat, judicial monotone: "… even if he was not aware that he had incurred a penalty." '

Culpeper looked pole-axed by this information. 'But be reasonable,' he whined. 'There must be some provision for making amends now that I am in full possession of the facts.'

'In most cases that may well be true,' I answered, 'but it is not within my gift to waive a Rule of golf. And what the Rule says is this: "… the player shall incur no penalty if he corrects his mistake before his opponent has played his next stroke. If the player fails so to correct the wrong information, he shall lose the hole." That last bit is in italics which I take it to mean that it is doubly important to impose such a penalty. I am truly sorry about that but there is nothing much I can do about it.'

'Well if you shared my view that the people who

framed this Rule and the whole rat-bag-full of separate match-play Rules are a bunch of reactionary cretins and that this particular instance represents a gross travesty of justice, then you could do the decent thing and offer me a half.'

An involuntary cry of anguish escaped my lips. 'Why, oh why, did you suggest that?' I pleaded. 'I was on the brink of making you that very offer in order to relieve your obvious distress. But now that you have raised the subject of a half I am forbidden from complying with my own dearest wish because such an action would clearly constitute an agreement to waive a Rule of Golf. Alas, you have precluded any possibility of a generous gesture on my part and I am left with no room to manoeuvre. You force me to accept the hole even though it offends against every bone in my body to prosper because of your innocent lapse.' I took out my handkerchief and covered my face so that Culpeper could not see the tears of sorrow that were welling up in my eyes.

For some reason Culpeper's game went to pot and I ran out a winner by six and five. I shall be most grateful, Mr Chairman, for your endorsement of my interpretation of the Rules on this occasion.

Yours faithfully,
Jas. Pontifex

18

FOR THOSE IN PERIL ON THE WATER HAZARD

Dear Chairman,

The reaction of some people to perfectly sane and sensible Rules of Golf is quite extraordinary. You tell them the Rule and they react as if you had insulted their intelligence as rational human beings. Take Mr Culpeper, normally amiable cove and – an important point in a golf club member – never slow to reach for his wallet in the men's bar. You could never accuse him of short arms and deep pockets. We were out yesterday in the gale that blew away the overnight rain storm and very exhilarating it was, too. Actually it became a bit too exhilarating for comfort when Culpeper put his ball into the lateral water hazard on the left of the seventh fairway. In point of fact the storm had made the stream overflow its banks and Culpeper's ball lay in about an inch of water but outside the line of red stakes defining the limit of the hazard. He was overjoyed to see where his ball lay, the poor booby, and remarked: 'Stroke of luck, that, landing in casual water instead of within the lateral water hazard. Now we take a nice free drop, and off we scamper, clippety-clop.'

You can imagine how I felt having to point out to him that it is incumbent upon the player in such circumstances to make a close examination of the topography of the water course and then make a rational analysis of the positioning of the red stakes. 'Now in this particular instance', I informed him, 'it is patently clear from the line of hydro-erosion that the natural boundary of the hazard runs along here. The Committee, or more likely that retarded youngster on the green staff – but since he was acting on the committee's behalf they have to carry the can – have made a complete nonsense of positioning the red stakes.'

'I've never seen water up as high as the line you call the natural boundary of the hazard.'

'Don't be so naive,' I reprimanded him. 'You know perfectly well that a hazard does not need to contain water in order to be defined as a water hazard. It is as clear as the nose on your face that those red stakes are several feet inside the margin of the hazard and must be ignored. You are not permitted to take advantage of the Committee's stupid error. Since it is quite clear that your ball is lying well within the natural boundary of the hazard I'm afraid that puts the kibosh on your sneaky little plan to take a free drop.'

'You mean that my ball, lying well outside the hazard, is, according to the fine print in some damn-fool Rule of Golf, inside the hazard. I simply don't believe it. I know and accept that in this lunatic game a moving ball can be deemed to be stationary, and a stationary ball can be deemed to be moving, and a ball sitting in clear view can be deemed to be lost, and a woman can be deemed to be a man, but you strain my credulity too far when you try to tell me that my ball sitting here is actually sitting over there, on the other side of the line of red stakes. I think you are pulling a fast one, you sanctimonious ratbag, and I'm calling your bluff. Show me in the Rule Book where my ball must be transmigrated from hither to yon.'

His cocky tone soon evaporated when I turned up the relevant entry in the book of Decisions on the Rules of Golf by the Royal and Ancient Golf Club of St Andrews and the United States Golf Association (Decision 26/2), which I just happened to have in my golf bag.

'That's just plain silly,' he whimpered.

I never gloat when I win a debating point, Mr Chairman, and I would be the last man on earth to throw someone's insults back into their face. But I must confess to experiencing a slight twinge of satisfaction at having upheld the forces of law and order in this instance.

'Shut up, pick up, drop and count one penalty stroke,' I commanded.

'I shall do nothing of the kind,' replied Culpeper. 'The ball is lying in shallow water and to a man of my capabilities it presents no great problem to release it from its watery thrall and send it soaring up the fairway.'

His decision to flout my instruction and select the rash option of playing the ball as it lay seemed to have restored his good spirits. He took his seven-iron and wound up for an almighty thrash at the ball. Somewhere along the way something went fearfully aglay. His left foot seemed to slip as he reached the top of his backswing and as he brought the club down he lost his footing altogether in the slimy mud and toppled over backwards as the club-head passed a foot above the ball travelling at about Mach 2.

Culpeper sat there and, like a noble liner on the slipway, slid slowly and gently into the depths of the swollen stream, laughing like a maniac.

In the circumstances I deemed it appropriate to suspend play while Culpeper repaired to the locker room for a quick shower and a change of clothing. As we were returning to the scene of the crime, Culpeper explained what had gone wrong with his attempted water recovery. The high wind was sending little waves across the surface of the water and as he started his take-away his club-head was impeded by contact with a wavelet.

You will have experienced this kind of thing a thousand times, Mr Chairman, and you know how it throws your swing completely out of kilter if your club touches something, maybe the thinnest of twigs, as you take it back. Accordingly, I expressed my sincere sympathy with Culpeper over this irritating misadventure. On reaching the spot and finding Culpeper's ball still *in situ*, he announced that this time, in the

'His left foot seemed to slip as he reached the top of his backswing...'

interests of putting a cap on his dry cleaning bills, he would take my advice and drop out of the hazard and accept the penalty stroke.

I have already indicated my internal torment at having to deem Culpeper's ball to be lying within the margin of the lateral water hazard and so you can perhaps imagine the laceration of my heart as I steeled myself to the painful duty of correcting him. I felt as if I was drowning a kitten as I said: 'Not one penalty stroke, my dear friend. Three.'

'Three!?' His shriek caused Colonel Rumbold to make an airshot two fairways away and, as it later transpired, the lady captain, fearful of some unseen horror such as a rampaging mad dog or another visitation by that streaker from the funny farm, locked herself in the toilet at the half-way house.

I explained the situation as calmly and politely as I could. 'Yes, three penalty strokes. When you tested the condition of the hazard with your club you incurred two penalty strokes...'

He interrupted me abruptly: 'When I did what?'

'When you tested the condition of the hazard. Rule 13-4. You just told me how the club-head caught up in a wave.'

'Well what has that got to do with testing the condition of the hazard?'

'That's what the Rule says. Clause b of 13-4 to be precise.' I handed him the Rule Book opened at page 42. He scanned the rule with a look of growing incredulity.

'And inadvertently touching the surface of the water is deemed to be testing it?'

'Certainly.'

'But testing it for what, for chrissake? Water is water. It never varies. You don't get thick water and thin water or powdery water or holding water. It's all the bloody same all over the world, two-thirds of which just happen to consist of water. There is no point in testing the stuff because we all know exactly what it's like.'

'The Rules of Golf allow me no latitude in the

interpretation of 13-4.' I replied. 'You may think this is a cretinous rule. That is your privilege. Even I may have certain reservations about it. Our opinions are completely irrelevant. So long as the Rule is in the Book so long we must all obey it, without cavil or question.'

'I'm not so sure about taking this lying down. When you have started your downstroke and you then abort your intention to strike the ball it does not count as a stroke. Right?'

'Quite correct.'

'Well I never had the slightest intention to test the condition of the hazard owing to the fact that I am quite familiar with the condition of water. The condition of water is wet. Period. Now if there is no evil intention there can be no crime. That is the very essence of English law as inherited from the Romans. No private club or association can make a rule which is at variance with the law of the land. Otherwise the chauvinistic Council of our golf club would make a rule empowering them to sell all the women members into concubinage. As a free born Englishman whose rights were enshrined in the Great Charter at Runnymede in the year of Our Lord 1215 I refuse to accept two penalty strokes for testing the condition of water, on the grounds that without intention there can be no sin, and, furthermore, that to admit to testing the condition of water would render me liable to incarceration in a padded cell.'

I was moved, Mr Chairman. Kenneth Branagh addressing the troops on the eve of Agincourt had nothing on Culpeper in full spate. And I think he might have a point, not that my humble opinions amount to a row of beans. It is for you to decide whether a two-stroke penalty may be waived on the grounds that the relevant Rule is both stupid and illegal.

Yours faithfully,
Jas. Pontifex

19

IDLE DALLIANCE WITH THE UNPLAYABLE RULE BOOK

Dear Chairman,

I must say I like the Sunningdale rule. This says that if a player asks his opponent if he may take relief from, say, ground under repair, a burrowing animal scrape, casual water or possibly a staked tree the answer has to be 'No.' In other words if there is the slightest scintilla of doubt in the player's mind about whether a free drop is in order, to a degree that he feels he should clear it with his opponent, then it is no go. Tough tit. Play it as it lies. I like that attitude. It is an absolute anathema to me the way some people are for ever trying to get out of problems of their own making by recourse to the Rules.

Mr Culpeper, my regular golfing companion, is a good friend and he can depend absolutely on my loyalty, but I must say he is a case in point. Since he has taken my advice to heart and now studies one Rule of Golf a night with its attendant Decisions before dropping off to sleep he has become an avaricious seeker after loopholes. This nightly immersion in the Book of Rules has had the effect of coarsening what was once a fine and sensitive mind. For example, whenever I am pondering a dubious lie, and resisting any temptation to seek his sanction for a free drop, he habitually comes over and remarks in a voice positively reeking of sarcasm: 'For God's sake piss on it and call it casual water so we can get on with the game.'

We were drawn to meet in the first round of the vets' cup and he threw the Rule Book at me on the very first green. When I went to mark my ball I discovered – quite the wrong word but press on regardless – that my lucky silver rouble could not be, as it were, discovered. Having no other article suitable for use as a ball-marker about my person, I therefore slipped off my glove and arranged it around my ball in a Churchillian V-for-victory confirmation, with the ball nestling between the two extended fingers. Confident that this adequately resolved my dilemma of having mislaid my regular ball-marker, and that I could replace my ball in its exact position, I picked up the ball.

Culpeper arranged his features in what can only be described as a picture of sneering smugness and announced: 'The Rules of Golf require that the ball be marked with a small coin or similar object. You may have read in the papers about the two-stroke penalty which was slapped on David Feherty in a tournament in Houston, which I might add for your benefit is in Texas, for marking his ball with a key. That was the general penalty for stroke-play, of course. This being match-play the general penalty is loss of hole.'

With that he picked up his ball.

As you can imagine, Mr Chairman, I came down on him like a ton of bricks. 'The Rules of Golf do not give specifications for the size, shape or weight of a ball-marker; they simply insist that a ball be marked in such a manner that it can be replaced precisely on its original spot. My glove did exactly that. There are extant Decisions sanctioning the use of a daisy, a club-head, a tee peg and a scratch in the surface of the green as permissible, albeit not entirely suitable, for marking a ball. So far as the Rules of Golf are concerned a key would be perfectly acceptable as a ball marker. Feherty was penalised under a PGA tournament rule. To the best of my knowledge, which I now confirm by scanning the sheet of local rules, this competition has not promulgated a local rule banning the use of gloves as ball-markers. Therefore, by picking up your ball in play without first marking it, you are

'I therefore slipped off my glove and arranged it around my ball ...'

subject to the match-play general penalty, which, as you correctly point out, is loss of hole. My hole I believe. Shall we proceed directly to the next tee?'

If looks could kill I would not be here to tell the tale, and I could see that Culpeper was determined to get his revenge. You will be familiar enough with our problem area alongside the sixth fairway where the rock comes so close to the surface that it is the devil's own job getting anything to grow there and the roots of the conifers snake around on the surface like the veins on a gigolo's neck when spurred on by a randy duchess. Culpeper drove over there and he called me across to observe his lie. His ball lay in a deep ravine between two roots. No man on earth could have got a club to it.

Culpeper addressed me in a tone of triumph: 'You will notice Mr Smarty Pants Rules Expert that the spot where we are standing is within a newly turfed area clearly marked with signs bearing the legend GUR, which, as I am sure you could have worked out for yourself, given time, stands for Ground Under Repair. Correct me if I am wrong but I do believe that I am entitled to a free drop from ground under repair. Furthermore, I draw your attention to the small depression in which my ball is cradled. The earth has been newly disturbed. What could have caused this depression or scrape? Do these little spherical pellets provide us with the vital clue? Surely they are the droppings of Brer Rabbit, a species of fauna recognised by the Rules of Golf as a burrowing animal. You are welcome to eat one if you doubt my conclusion. And I am confident that you will endorse my contention that a player is entitled to a free drop from the scrape of a burrowing animal. In addition, I invite you to inspect the accumulation of liquid which is clearly visible around my ball. I do believe it is water of the casual ilk, as you may test for yourself if you so wish by dipping your finger in it and licking it. I feel sure you will discover that it is not Johnny Walker Black Label and that, furthermore, you will not demur when I suggest that a free drop is available from casual water. So here we have a triple whammy, Mr Candy-Ass Rules Man, a three-way entitlement to a free drop. Even you couldn't talk me out of my just deserts this time.'

So saying, he snatched up his ball and said: 'We will do this down to the last dot and comma of the Rule. So you tell me. Where do I drop it?'

Throughout this diatribe my face had been a mask of impassivity and I had not uttered a word. I now recited flatly: 'Rule 28 requires that you shall, under penalty of one stroke, play your next stroke as nearly as possible at the spot from which the ball was last played; or drop a ball within two clubs' lengths of the spot where the ball lay, but not nearer the hole. In this instance, that option would surely put your ball into play in ground under repair and you would then be entitled to free relief from that condition; or you can drop a ball behind the point where the ball lay, keeping that point directly between the hole and the spot on which the ball is dropped, with no limit to how far behind that point the ball may be dropped.'

For a moment I honestly feared that my old friend was going to have a seizure. He had turned crimson and was experiencing considerable difficulty in controlling violent spasms which racked his frame. He seemed to have lost the gift of speech but eventually spluttered: 'But that's the unplayable ball rule. I'm not declaring my ball unplayable when I have three, yes three, impeccable claims to a free drop.'

By way of emphasis he thrust three fingers into my face. For a moment I thought he was going to stick them up my nose. I'm sure he would have done if I'd had three nostrils.

'We have here what we Candy-Ass Rules Men sometimes call a triple whammy,' I remarked as I led him back to the original site of his ball among the tree roots. 'You are an experienced enough golfer to recognise that this ball is physically impossible to hit with a golf club. It is beyond a peradventure unplayable.'

He started to interrupt: 'But, but ...' I silenced him with a gesture and continued: 'Since the ball is unplayable that fact supersedes all other considerations and overrides all rights to relief from unusual ground conditions. You have no choice in the matter, just as I have no authority to waive a Rule of Golf. The only way you can continue the match is to deem your ball unplayable and proceed under the provisions of Rule 28.' I handed him the book, opened at the relevant passage, and we moved on.

Culpeper's heart was not in it. His spirit was crushed and the fire had died in his breast. He played like a zombie and I went six up with six to play without doing anything special. On the thirteenth tee he made a listless swing and the club-head almost passed clean under the ball, making contact only with the rounded plateau, if that is not a contradiction in terms, which bears the maker's name on the top of the club-head. The ball popped almost vertically into the air and plummeted down on to the high, pulpit tee of the seventh hole. The ball rolled to the edge of the tee, toppled over the rim and bounced plink, plonk, plink, plonk down the rustic wooden steps which the green staff built. The ball came to rest on the fifth step.

'That's an artificial structure, right?' said Culpeper in a sepulchral monotone.

'Right,' said I.

'So I take relief from an immovable obstruction, right?' he asked.

'Wrong,' said I.

'Why the f-f-f-flaming hell not? Just because it is my ball, I suppose.'

'You must not get paranoid about the Rules of Golf. They are not out to get you personally. They are quite impartial. Why do you think your ball stopped on the fifth step? Nobody rescinded the law of gravity just to spite you. No, the wooden tread of the fifth step has come adrift and is, as you may observe, lying at the foot of the banking. Your ball's downward progress was arrested because it landed on soft earth and did not bounce. It is just what we golfers call a rub of the green that since your ball lies on a natural surface, rather than on an artificial surface made by man, you get no relief and must play it as it lies. In the wrong direction, I fancy, unless you reverse a club and take a whack at it left-handed.'

Culpeper gave me a blank stare, raised his arms and said: 'Kamerad! I know when I'm beat.'

The Rules of Golf urge us to be absolutely specific and unambiguous in making verbal concessions of a putt, a hole or a match. Culpeper's declaration was ungrammatical but I felt it was an inopportune moment to correct his tenses. It was also capable of different interpretations but in making this submission, Mr Chairman, I hope you will accept that his intended meaning was a concession of the match. In support of this contention I might add that he wandered off in the direction of the club house. True he did not observe the convention of shaking me by the hand and thanking me for a keen and well fought match, but I got the impression he was preoccupied with his own private thoughts.

Yours faithfully,

Jas. Pontifex

20

A RARE BIT OF
HOW'S-YER-FATHER
INTERRUPTUS

Dear Chairman,

As a layman I hesitate to poke my untutored nose into the labyrinthine gallimaufry which goes under the generic title of The Law. But I am still entitled to an opinion and I wonder whether you, who are a thousand times better qualified to reach an educated conclusion on the subject, would endorse my view that the Rules of Golf Committees cannot possibly have a mandate to legislate for people, animals, events and objects beyond the boundaries of the golf course and therefore, as I would aver, outside their sphere of influence.

I refer specifically, as you must surely have guessed already, to the anomaly, as I perceive it to be, that a movable artificial object sited out of bounds may be removed but that no relief is permissible from an immovable artificial object out of bounds. The very terminology of the Rule suggests to me that the committees are not entirely sure of their rights in this context, slightly uneasy about overstepping the mark as they venture over the boundary fence.

I mean, 'artificial object' is not a golf expression. Within the boundary of the golf course such objects would be termed movable or immovable obstructions. Even the golfer's inalienable right to stand out of bounds in order to play a ball lying in bounds hints at a conspiracy between the player and the Rules of Golf

Committee to commit an act of trespass, a civil offence as I understand it, or tort in your legal jargon, but carrying a punitive sanction nonetheless. Moving an artificial object which lies out of bounds could very well constitute a criminal act; and in that case would the Rules of Golf Committee, or possibly the golf club itself, be held equally culpable for aiding and abetting a felony? You may think that these hypothetical questions might make for an interesting debate in the men's bar one winter's evening between masters of jurisprudence, much as the ancient philosphers debated how many angels could dance on the head of a pin. But the reason I raise this subject is because of the immediate practicalities of actual and tragic events, involving real people, right here, on the boundary of our golf course, as recently as three days ago. Your first question may well be to enquire why it took so long to report a dispute involving the Rules of Golf to your good self. In reply, Mr Chairman, I have to confess that it took some time to arrange bail. But that is getting slightly ahead of the story.

You know that place in the woods where the fifth fairway runs alongside the B207 and the milk tanker ran amok and took out twenty yards of our stone wall? Well, Mr Culpeper and I were playing a qualifying round for the vets' cup and he carved his drive away into that clearing and we found his ball sitting pretty an inch or so inside the white OB posts. The snag was that a black Mini-Cooper was backed right up to our boundary, making it impossible for Culpeper to stand to the ball or, indeed, get a club to it. The car, I may say, was a very flash affair with all the goodies: turbo-charger, go-faster stripes, tinted glass windows and about eight extraneous fog lights bolted on the front. There was no sign of the driver; probably off blackberrying, I opined.

Culpeper confirmed with me that he was entitled to stand out of bounds in order to play his ball lying in bounds. He then enquired about the status of the Mini and I explained to him all that rigmarole about artificial objects, movable and immovable.

'By what measure do you distinguish between the movable and the immovable?' he asked.

'That judgment must be purely pragmatic,' I told him. 'If you can move an artificial object, then it automatically becomes, by definition, a movable artificial object.'

I know what you are thinking, Mr Chairman. The Rules of Golf say nothing about how one distinguishes between the movability or otherwise of artificial objects. In this instance I acted on the basis of presumptive logic and applied the terms and conditions governing movable and immovable obstructions to artificial objects. I am very well aware that they are not identical entities, otherwise a player would be entitled to relief from an artificial object lying out of bounds. But I used the only points of reference available to me.

'May I enlist the assistance of spectators, fellow competitors, officials and passers-by in lifting an artificial object, thereby rendering what would otherwise be an immovable artificial object a movable artificial object?'

Since the only pertinent category in this instance was that of fellow competitor and, as I explained to Culpeper, my doctor had expressly forbidden me to lift heavy weights, the answer was 'Yes', but it was also totally irrelevant.

Culpeper remarked that if only we could get into the car it would be child's play to push it clear. He tried the driver's door and then walked round the back of the car to the passenger's door. No joy. Then, to my amazement, he stood gazing upward and sucking in huge gulps of air. He was making curious little grunting sounds as he suddenly bent his knees, with a very straight back and his bottom sticking out in the approved weight-lifting style. He thrust his hands under the sill and with a roar of exertion and triumph he straightened his legs and flipped the Mini over onto its back. It was an extraordinary feat of strength and I congratulated him on it when we were in the cell that evening, but he said the actual weight was no big deal for a trained lifter.

'It was an extraordinary feat of strength...'

He now had a clear stance but no opportunity to avail himself of it because of the pandemonium which had broken out inside the Mini, whence came screams of outrage, fear and pain, both male and female. I am no prude, as you know Mr Chairman, and I am as broad-minded as the next man. But I was simply unable to give credence to the suspicion that was prompted by the uproar and the occasional word I was able to distinguish. I mean to say. In the back of a Mini? Is it physically possible? Then we heard the male voice shouting into a mobile telephone and giving instructions about the car's whereabouts.

I was all for slinking quietly away but Culpeper would have none of it. 'I have done nothing wrong. I have complied meticulously with the Rules and regulations and I intend to play the shot to which I am entitled.'

That is when we heard the sirens, followed in short order by a Fire Service truck marked 'Rescue And Emergency Squad', an ambulance and a police car. The sergeant knew sweet Fanny Adams about golf and absolutely refused to listen to my explanation about the distinctions between movable and immovable artificial objects. He insisted we return with him to the station for questioning.

If Chief Inspector Habgood had been there, or any of the coppers from J Division who enjoy the courtesy of our course, I daresay the whole affair would have been sorted in minutes. But the people who dealt with our case were either ignorant about golf or actively opposed to the game. Of course, my solicitor, who also acts for Culpeper, would be on holiday, wouldn't he? They questioned us for ages and ages and then said we would be held at the police station pending a report from the hospital on the injuries to the couple. The sex-crazed owner of the Mini turned out to be a nephew of the Chief Constable, would you believe?

We were in and out of the interview room all next day. They were preparing to nail us on charges of malicious damage to property, to wit one customised

Mini-Cooper de luxe; assault occasioning actual bodily harm; behaviour calculated to cause a breach of the peace – a totally spurious accusation, that, because it is all to do with peeping toms and the entire incident was caused because we did *not* peep inside the car; and obstructing a police officer in the execution of his duty – that was Culpeper calling the sergeant an ignorant, officious prat. They clearly intended to throw the book at us with a vengeance.

I trust that anything said by a golfer to the Chairman of the Tournament Committee is classified as a privileged communication, like the information from a sinner to his priest in the confessional, because it was a condition of our discharge, a word of honour job rather than a legal undertaking, you understand, that we keep this information strictly to ourselves. But it turns out that the woman in the Mini was none other than the wife of our local MP. You know the one; she came here with her husband for the opening of the new extension to the clubhouse. I remember now that Roger the Dodger Hawkins warned us not to be fooled by that look as if butter wouldn't melt in her mouth; 'Mark my words,' he said, 'that one's a bit of a goer.' Seems he was all too right.

Anyway, they booted us out into the street at two o'clock in the morning and said that on this occasion there would be no charges.

In the light of the above events, Mr Chairman, are we permitted to resume our disrupted round or should it be washed out and the round replayed?

Yours faithfully,
Jas. Pontifex

21

THE SLIPPERY SLOPE
TO PERDITION

Dear Chairman,

You will remember St Simeon's Club out on the Woking road: lovely old clubhouse, decent grub and a very fine club claret. Typical Surrey heath course, all heather and silver birch and pine trees. You were Chairman of the Up-and-Downers when we had a meeting there a couple of years ago and you made a frightfully witty speech when you referred to the 'fir-cone golf course' where you couldn't hit your 'fir-cone hat' to save your 'fir-cone life'.

Mr Culpeper was not there on that occasion, not being a member of our select band. I have, as you know, put him up to the Committee for consideration although, after what happened yesterday, I am not sure he is entirely a suitable candidate for the Up-and-Downers. It is very important, as I am sure you will agree, that the society maintains the highest standards and ensures that new memebers are completely good eggs. I shall defer to your expert judgment, as always, but I rather fancy that when you hear the sordid details of the episode I am about to relate you will have reservations about the goodness of the Culpeper egg. You may well concur with my suspicion that if dropped into a bowl of water Culpeper would bob up to the surface and float.

It was like this. I had regaled Culpeper with tales of the golfing delights and scrummy tuck available at St Simeon's until he was positively slavering at the mouth and imploring me to arrange a day out. His wish, of course, was my command and we decided to play a medal round in the morning for handicapping purposes, the high man to pay for lunch. All went reasonably well and after sixteen holes I was a stroke up on him – or should that be down, being the lower score? – and wondering whether I could swing the pre-prandial g-and-t onto the Culpeper's lunch tab when it all started to go wrong. I really nailed my drive down the seventeenth fairway, every inch of 160 yards, and then, just as I was at the top of my backswing for the approach shot, some dashed bird burst into a cacophony of squawking and shrieking. I nearly jumped out of my boots and the ball hooked high up on the bank among the pine trees alongside the green. My mood was not exactly improved by Culpeper's enquiry as to whether I did not agree that the song of the thrush was the finest expression of nature's bounty. Mind you, I make no complaint against Culpeper – yet. His question was innocent enough in all conscience; the man does not have the subtlety to engage in sophisticated verbal gamesmanship.

I managed to climb up that steep ascent, though not without considerable effort, because the ground was thickly carpeted with old pine needles which provided only the most treacherous of footings. The ball was sitting cleanly on a thick mat of pine needles, absolutely pin-high as you would expect of a downy old bird with the keenest eye for distance in the club, even though I say so myself. For once I had a gap and theoretically I could clip the ball cleanly straight down to the flag.

I took my stance with the greatest care because the angle of the slope made my position precarious enough, never mind the hazardous nature of the conditions underfoot. As I did my usual little shimmy, which is part of my routine for taking the address position, I froze with horror because that thick accumulation of pine needles began to slide down the hill. It was rather like standing on a raft just as it begins to go over Niagara Falls. I held my breath as it gathered speed and when we hit the swale alongside the green

'It was rather like standing on a raft as it begins to go over Niagara Falls...'

I fell arse over tip and my ball did likewise, popping forwards onto the green – and damn me if it didn't roll straight into the hole!

Culpeper was lying three in the bunker on the other side of the green and I was down in two! He was wetting himself with hysterical laughter at my undignified recumbency in a nest of pine needles, 'like a broody old hen', as he put it. I made a mental note to hit him for a double Remy to top off my free lunch.

Then the unspeakable swine came out with his vile heresy: 'If the ball moves at the address the player is deemed to have caused it to move. Penalty stroke. The ball must be replaced in its original position. So back you go up the bank. Let's see you do another slalom. You will be playing four – and paying for lunch as well, I'll be bound.'

I was dumbfounded, Mr Chairman. Granted my ball had changed position but it had not moved one iota within the meaning of the Act. This was directly analagous with a ball firmly lodged in the fork of branch which is waving in the breeze. It has, as you know, been ruled that in such circumstances, where the ball does not move in relation to its immediate surroundings, then it is deemed not to have moved or be moving. The same applies to a ball being borne along in moving water. My ball had not changed position in relation to its immediate surrounds throughout the descent and when those immediate surroundings ran up against the shoulder of the green the stationary-moving ball continued its journey across the green under the influence of the inertial momentum derived from the force of gravity which is not, as you and I understand perfectly well, an outside agency. The position, I submit, is exactly the same as if the ball had simply rolled down the bank into the hole before I got to it.

I will draw a veil over the subsequent exchange of views and the summary cancellation of our luncheon arrangements, since they are neither pertinent nor seemly. I simply ask that you ignore the annotation which Culpeper scribbled on my card and that you endorse my score of two for the seventeenth hole and pass the amended card to the Handicapping Committee.

Yours faithfully,

Jas. Pontifex

22

THE TURNING
OF THE WORM

Dear Chairman,

As a student of human nature, you will be familiar with the paradox that the mildest, most even-tempered of men become the most violent of men, given to uncontrollable rages, when they finally snap. The longer I play with Mr Culpeper the more I am aware of this quirk of human behaviour, and I am sorry to say that the Rules of Golf seem frequently to be the catalyst for his uncharacteristic rages. I cannot tell you how many times I have impressed on him that there is no point in railing against what he perceives to be injustices in the Rules. An air of insouciance, a wry smile, a brave stoicism, a quiet determination never to infringe this Rule again – these, I tell him, are the appropriate responses as the stern lash of 18-2a/7 lacerates the flesh.

   The men who make the Rules, I assure him, are not engaged in some vile conspiracy to drive him out of his mind, even though it may seem like it at times, and it is no use kicking against the pricks. I had occasion to deliver a homily along these lines yet again this morning during the monthly medal when Mr Culpeper had the misfortune to five-putt the seventh green, easily enough done on that switchback putting surface, as we have all discovered to our cost at some time or other.

   He was miffed, and understandably so, as anyone with my generosity of spirit would readily admit. I was rather less inclined to charity as we walked onto the eighth tee where he punished his disobedient putter by delivering a frightful smack with it against the tee box. Poetic justice was done, however. The head was severely bent out of kilter. He tried bending it straight by hammering it with his wedge, using the tee box as an anvil, until I stopped him with a shake of an admonitory finger.

'Let the pro repair it after we finish,' I said. 'After all, you cannot use it again during the round.'

He glared and growled through clenched teeth: 'I am perfectly well aware that I cannot replace this blasted, benighted bludgeon because it did not become damaged during the course of normal play. But there is nothing in the Rules of Golf, you sanctimonious prat, to forbid me wrapping this putter around your scrawny neck if you try to pull one of your rulesmanship strokes on me.'

A conciliatory approach was clearly called for. At that moment I was reminded of that wise man, it may even have been your good self, Chair, who declared that to understand is to forgive. I addressed Culpeper accordingly:

'The great Bobby Jones remarked that we learn only from our mistakes and I implore you to treat this incident as a learning experience, for it is in that spirit of helpfulness that I must inform you of the provisions of Rule 4-2: "If the playing characteristics of a player's club are changed because of damage sustained other than in the normal course of play, the club shall not subsequently be used during the round." Although all my instincts of friendship and sportsmanship urge me to let you use my putter for the rest of the round, alas the Rules do not permit such Samaritan brotherhood.'

'You're enjoying this, aren't you?' he snarled. 'You're no better than those pricks you were saying I shouldn't kick.'

For reasons which are not strictly pertinent to the case in point, Culpeper's five putts on the seventh did not cause him to lose the honour; he therefore had no opportunity to reflect on the error of his ways in quiet tranquillity while I went through my teeing-off routine. As a result he was still incandescent with rage as he seized his driver and positively leaped onto the tee.

The violence of his assault on the ball was wondrous to behold. I estimate that his club-head entered the turf some eleven inches short of the ball at a descending angle of attack. The club-head continued its inexorable advance like a snow plough, causing a thick-ish slice of rural Surrey to curl clear over the teed ball. The dying impetus of the club-head just dislodged the ball from its perch and it sat there in pristine splendour under its arch of turf. But not for long. With a fearsome oath Culpeper bent down and snatched at the strip of turf so violently that he detached it completely from the tee.

'Provided that they are not fixed or growing. Rule 23.' I intoned quietly. 'Two strokes.'

He threw the divot down into its scrape and hammered it home with his driver.

'Improving line of play. Rule 13. Two strokes.' I whispered.

He picked up his ball.

'Ball in play purposely touched by player. Rule 18-2. One stroke.' I commented.

Then he replaced the ball on its tee and gave it a fearful whack on a high, slicing flight into the lake.

'Ball played from wrong place. Rule 20. Minimum two strokes, maybe disqualification.'

'What the hell are you chuntering about, you diseased wart-hog?' he demanded.

'I am merely trying to help you keep a true and accurate record of your score for submission to the Committee,' I replied with as much dignity as I could muster in these distressing circumstances.

'I don't need any supercilious git to tell me that I lie one, in the bottom of that stinking cess pit they call a pond,' he yelled.

'*Au contraire*,' I responded with a disarming smile. 'Remember that I am trying to help you become a better golfer and a more contented man by profiting from your minor peccadillos. Subject to ratification by the Committee, I make it that after adding the penalty

'The violence of his assault on the ball was
wondrous to behold.'

stroke for gaining relief from the water hazard, your next stroke will be your tenth.'

His eyes flashed, with enlightenment, or so I presume. He advanced on me with outstretched arms, obviously intent on enfolding me in a friendly embrace of gratitude for my solicitous endeavours to improve his knowledge of the Rules. But he must have stubbed his toe or something because he sort of stumbled towards me and, but for a timely body swerve such as baffled the opposition in my days as a will o' the wisp centre for the school colts XV, I fear the hands intending to clasp me warmly around the shoulders would have made violent contact in the region of my neck.

His unimpeded progress carried him into sharp collision with his clubs and trolley, which collapsed beneath him. Having satisfied myself that his injuries were superficial, although undoubtedly painful, and that he would be able to disentangle himself without outside assistance, I deemed it prudent to remove myself from the scene at this juncture.

I am, of course, fully conversant with Rule 6-8 and am aware of my duty to report to you as soon as practicable and give reasons for my suspension of play without specific permission. I am further sensible of the fact that my reasons must be satisfactory and that the members of the Rules of Golf Committee take full satisfaction from nothing less than broken bones or serious illness. Happily, I suffered neither on this occasion but trust the circumstances I have described will nevertheless be deemed to be acceptable justification for my premature return to the clubhouse.

Yours faithfully,
Jas. Pontifex